Suicide Thoughts and Reflections, 1960-1980

A SPECIAL ISSUE OF
Suicide and Life-Threatening Behavior

by
Edwin S. Shneidman

 **HUMAN SCIENCES PRESS, INC.**
72 Fifth Avenue   3 Henrietta Street
NEW YORK, NY 10011 ● LONDON, WC2E 8LU

100613

Library of Congress Catalog Number 81-81844
ISBN: 0-89885-090-8
Copyright 1981 by Human Sciences Press

HUMAN SCIENCES PRESS
72 Fifth Avenue
New York, New York 10011

Printed in the United States of America

Table of Contents

Preface

This book contains ten pieces on suicide written between 1960 and 1980. The contents are identical with those contained in the special Winter, 1981 issue of *Suicide and Life-Threatening Behavior*—my last issue as Editor, after eleven years. It was my hope to give members of the American Association of Suicidology a sampling, in one place, of some of my writings on this topic over the past twenty years. I am planning a similar volume for the year 2,000.

For this volume I have selected pieces representative of my past writings on suicide. In these selections I have tried to illustrate the multiple — the cognitive, affective, psycho-dynamic, socio-cultural, and philosophic — aspects of self-destructive phenomena. My current mood is to emphasize the primacy of the psycho-dynamic view, to keep a constant eye on the philosophic-existential orientation of the person, but to place a special emphasis on the person's thinking styles — always in an attempt to combine theoretical and clinical efforts.

The following people have most directly fostered, stimulated or shaped my suicidological career and I am happy now to acknowledge my real debt to each of them: Jacques Choron, Theodore J. Curphey, Norman Farberow, Loma Feigenberg, Paul Friedman, Harry M. Grayson, Milton Greenblatt, Harold M. Hildreth, Evelyn Hooker, Robert E. Litman, Karl A. Menninger, Jerome Motto, Henry A. Murray, Robert R. Sears, Erwin Stengel, Avery Weisman, Louis J. West and Stanley Yolles.

E.S.S.
UCLA
November, 1981

Suicide

No one really knows why human beings commit suicide. Indeed, the very person who takes his own life may be least aware at the moment of decision of the essence (much less the totality) of his reasons and emotions for doing so. At the outset, it can be said that a dozen individuals can kill themselves and "do" (or commit) 12 psychologically different deeds. Understanding suicide—like understanding any other complicated human act such as drug or alcohol misuse or antisocial behavior—involves insights drawn from many fields that touch on man's entire psychological and social life.

Definition of Suicide

In this article the definition of suicide will be treated in two ways; first, a definition is put forward and, then, some of the difficulties and complexities involved in defining the term are discussed. Briefly defined, suicide is the human act of self-inflicted, self-intentioned cessation.

Suicide is not a disease (although there are those who think so); it is not, in the view of the most detached observers, an immorality (although, as noted below, it has often been so treated in Western and other cultures); and, finally, it is unlikely that any one theory will ever explain phenomena as varied and as complicated as human self-destructive behaviors. In general, it is probably accurate to say that suicide always involves an individual's tortured and tunneled logic in a state of inner-felt, intolerable emotion. In addition, this mixture of constricted thinking and unbearable anguish is infused with that individual's conscious and unconscious psychodynamics (of hate, dependency, hope, etc.), playing themselves out within a social and cultural context, which itself imposes various degrees of restraint on, or facilitation of, the suicidal act.

From the *Encyclopaedia Britannica*, 1973 printing of the 14th Edition, Vol. 21, pp. 383-385 (7 pages). Reprinted with permission of William Benton, publishers.

This definition implies that committing suicide involves a conceptualization of death; that it combines an individual's conscious
wish to be dead and his action to carry out that wish; that is focuses
on his intention (which may have to be inferred by others); that the
goal of action relates to death (rather than self-injury or self-
mutilation); and that it focuses on the concept of the cessation of
the individual's conscious, introspective life. The word "suicide"
would seem to be clear enough, although such phrases as "self-
inflicted" (in the incident in which Saul asked another soldier to
kill him) and "self-intentioned" (when Seneca was ordered by Nero
to kill himself) add to the complications of finding a clear-cut
definition of suicide.

Complexities and Difficulties with Definitions

If the definition of suicide is complicated, there are even more
confusions of meaning when the adjective "suicidal" is used. Some
of the current confusions relating to the term "suicidal" are as
follows:

1. The word "suicidal" is used to cover a number of categories of
   behavior. For example, it may convey the idea that an individual has committed suicide, attempted suicide, threatened suicide, exhibited depressive behavior—with or without suicidal
   ideation—or manifested generally self-destructive or inimical
   patterns.
2. There also is confusion with respect to the temporal aspects of
   suicidal acts. One sees "suicidal" used to convey the information
   that an individual was self-destructive, is currently self-
   destructive, or will be so. Most diagnoses in this field are post
   hoc definitions, labeling an individual as "suicidal" only after
   he or she has attempted or committed suicide.
3. Serious confusion relating to suicidal phenomena may occur if
   the individual's intentions in relation to his own cessation are
   not considered. "Suicide" may be defined for medical, legal, and
   administrative purposes. In the United States and Great Britain
   (and most of the countries reporting to the World Health Organization), suicide is defined (by a medical examiner or coroner) as
   one of four possible modes of death. There are 140 possible
   causes of death but only four modes. An acronym for the four
   modes of death is N-A-S-H: natural, accident, suicide, and
   homicide. This traditional fourfold classification of all deaths

leaves much to be desired. Its major deficiency is that it emphasizes relatively adventitious details in the death. Whether the
individual is invaded by a lethal virus (natural), or a lethal
bullet (homicide), or a lethal steering wheel (accident) may be a
trivial difference to the deceased, who may be more interested in
the date of his death. More importantly, the N-A-S-H classification of death erroneously treats the human being in Cartesian
fashion, as a biological machine, rather than appropriately
treating him as a motivated psychosocial organism. It also
obscures the individual's intentions in relation to his own
cessation and, further, completely neglects the contemporary
concepts of psychodynamic psychology regarding intention,
purpose, and the multiple determination of behavior including
unconscious motivation.

It may make more sense eventually to eschew the category of
suicide entirely—along with the other N-A-S-H categories—and
instead to classify all deaths in terms of the role of the individual in
his own demise: (1) intentioned, (2) subintentioned—cases in which
an individual has played partial, latent, covert, or unconscious
roles in hastening his own demise—or (3) unintentioned. The
problems of certification would then be no more difficult than they
are at present, but such a classification would serve to put man
back into his own dying and death and, in addition, would reflect
the 20th-century view of man that emphasizes both the conscious
and unconscious aspects of his intentionality.

The Word

Suicide is a relatively recent word. According to *The Oxford
English Dictionary*, the word was first used in 1651 by Walter
Charleton when he said, interestingly enough, "To vindicate ones
self from ... inevitable Calamity, by Sui-cide is not ... a Crime."
The exact date of its first use is open to some question. Edward
Phillips in the 1662 edition of his dictionary, *A New World in
Words*, claimed invention of the word: "One barbarous word I shall
produce, which is suicide." Curiously enough he does not derive it
from the death of oneself but says it "should be derived from 'a
sow' ... since it is a swinish part for a man to kill himself."
The British poetry critic Alfred Alvarez in 1971 claimed that he
found the word was used even earlier, in Sir Thomas Browne's
Religio Medici, written in 1635 and published in 1642, in the

following passage: "Herein are they not extreme that can allow a man to be his own assassin and so highly extoll the end by suicide of Cato."

The word "suicide" does not appear in Robert Burton's *Anatomy of Melancholy* (1652 edition) nor in Samuel Johnson's *Dictionary* (1755). Before the introduction of the word, other terms, mostly circumlocutions and euphemisms relating to self-murder, were used—among them self-destruction, self-killing, self-slaughter, *sibi mortem consciecere* (to procure one's own death), *vim sibi inferre* (to cause violence to oneself), and *sui manu cadere* (to fall by one's own hand). Burton's phrases for suicide include "to make way with themselves" and "they offer violence to themselves." The traditional (and current) German term is *Selbstmord*—self-murder.

It may well be that in light of current concepts and facts about human self-destruction a new (and more accurate) term may eventually come into general usage. In the 1960s a relatively new word, suicidology, was introduced. *Suicidologie* was used in a text by a Dutch professor, W.A. Bonger, in 1929, but did not become widely known. Independently, the word was used by Shneidman in a book review (1964) and then in the *Bulletin of Suicidology* (1967) and at the first convention of the American Association of Suicidology, which met in 1968. Since then the word has come into general use. Suicidology is defuned as the scientific study of suicidal phenomena.

Main Threads of Suicidal Study

The modern era of the study of suicide began around the turn of the 20th century, with two main threads of investigation, the sociological and the psychological, associated with the names of Émile Durkheim (1858-1917) and Sigmund Freud (1856-1939), respectively. Much earlier, during classical Greek times, suicide was viewed in various ways, but in classical Rome, in the centuries just before the Christian era, life was held rather cheaply and suicide was viewed either neutrally or even positively. The Roman Stoic Seneca said: "Living is not good, but living well. The wise man, therefore, lives as well as he should, not as long as he can. . . . He will always think of life in terms of quality not quantity. . . . Dying early or late is of no relevance, dying well or ill is . . . even if it is true that while there is life there is hope, life is not to be bought at any cost."

Historically it seems that the excessive martyrdom and penchant toward suicide of the early Christians frightened the church elders sufficiently for them to introduce a serious deterrent. That constraint was to relate suicide to crime and the sin associated with crime. A major change occurred in the 4th century with a categorical rejection of suicide by St. Augustine (354-430). Suicide was considered a crime, because it precluded the possibility of repentance and because it violated the Sixth Commandment relating to killing. Suicide was a greater sin than any sin one might wish to avoid. This view was elaborated by St. Thomas Aquinas (1225-74), who emphasized that suicide was a mortal sin in that it usurped God's power over man's life and death. Although neither the Old nor the New Testament directly forbids suicide, by 693 the Council of Toledo proclaimed that an individual who attempted suicide was to be excommunicated. The notion of suicide as sin took firm hold and for hundreds of years played an important part in Western man's view of self-destruction.

The Christian injunctions against suicide seemed paradoxically to rest on a respect for life (especially the life of the soul in the hereafter) and were a reaction to the light way in which life was held by the Romans. If those were the church's original motivations, however, they went awry and the results were excessive and counterproductive, and resulted in degrading, defaming, impoverishing, torturing, and persecuting individuals (who had attempted suicide, committed suicide, or were the survivors) whom they had originally tried to protect and succor.

The French philosopher Jean Jacques Rousseau (1712-78), by emphasizing the natural state of man, transferred sin from man to society, making man generally good (and innocent) and asserting that it is society that makes him bad. The disputation as to the locus of blame—whether in man or in society—is a major theme that dominates the history of suicidal thought. David Hume (1711-76) was one of the first major Western philosophers to discuss suicide in the absence of the concept of sin. His famous essay "On Suicide," published in 1777, a year after his death, was promptly suppressed. That well-reasoned essay is a statement of the Enlightenment position on suicide. The burden of the essay is to refute the view that suicide is a crime; it does so by arguing that suicide is not a transgression of our duties to God, to our fellow citizens, or to ourselves. He states that ". . . prudence and courage should engage us to rid ourselves at once of existence when it becomes a burden. . . . If it be no crime in me to divert the Nile or Danube from its course, were I able to effect such purposes, where then is the crime in turning a few ounces of blood from their natural channel?"

Whereas Hume tried to decriminalize suicide, Rousseau turned the blame from man to society. In the 20th century, the two giants of suicidal theorizing played rather different roles: Durkheim focused on society's inimical effects on the individual, while Freud—eschewing the notions of either sin or crime—gave suicide back to man but put the locus of action in man's unconscious.

Durkheim's best-known work, *Le Suicide* (1897), established a model for sociological investigations of suicide. There have been many subsequent studies of this genre. The monographs and books by R.S. Cavan on suicide in Chicago (1926), of Calvin F. Schmid on suicide in Seattle (1928) and Minneapolis (1933), of Peter Sainsbury on suicide in London (1955), of Louis I. Dublin and Bessie Bunzel (1933), and of Andrew F. Henry and James F. Short, Jr., on suicide in the U.S. (1954) all fall within the sociological tradition of taking a plot of ground—a city or a country—and figuratively or literally reproducing its map several times to show its socially shady (and topographically shaded) areas and their differential relationships to suicide rates.

According to Durkheim suicide is the result of society's strength or weakness of control over the individual. He posited three basic types of suicide, each a result of man's relationship to his society. In one instance, the "altruistic" suicide is literally required by society. Here, the customs or rules of the group demand suicide under certain circumstances. Hara-kiri and suttee are examples of altruistic suicides. In such instances, however, the persons had little choice. Self-inflicted death was honorable; continuing to live was ignominious. Society dictated their action and, as individuals, they were not strong enough to defy custom.

Most suicides in the United States are "egoistic"—Durkheim's second category. Contrary to the circumstances of an altruistic suicide, egoistic suicide occurs when the individual has too few ties with his community. Demands, in this case to live, do not reach him. Thus, proportionately, more individuals, especially men, who are on their own kill themselves than do church or family members.

Finally, Durkheim called "anomic" those suicides that occur when the accustomed relationship between an individual and his society is suddenly shattered. The shocking, immediate loss of a job, a close friend, or a fortune is thought sufficient to precipitate anomic suicides; or, conversely, poor men surprised by sudden wealth also have been shocked into anomic suicide.

The students and followers of Durkheim include Maurice Halb-
wachs in France and Ronald W. Maris and Jack D. Douglas in the
United States. Douglas, especially, has argued that Durkheim's
constructs came not so much from the facts of life and death as
from official statistics, which themselves may distort the very facts
they are supposed to report.

As Durkheim detailed the sociology of suicide, so Freud fathered
psychological explanations. To him, suicide was essentially within
the mind. Since men ambivalently identify with the objects of their
own love, when they are frustrated the aggressive side of the
ambivalence will be directed against the internalized person. The
main psychoanalytical position on suicide was that it represented
unconscious hostility directed toward the introjected (ambivalently
viewed) love object. For example, one killed oneself in order to
murder the image of one's loved-hated father within one's breast.
Psychodynamically, suicide was seen as murder in the 180th degree.

In an important exegesis of Freud's thoughts on suicide by
Robert E. Litman (1967, 1970), he traces the development of Freud's
thoughts on the subject, taking into account Freud's clinical experiences and his changing theoretical positions from 1881 to 1939. It is
evident from Litman's analysis that there is more to the psychodynamics of suicide than hostility. These factors include the general
features of human condition in Western civilization, specifically,
suicide-prone mechanisms involving rage, guilt, anxiety, dependency, and a great number of specifically predisposing conditions.
The feelings of helplessness, hopelessness, and abandonment are
very important.

Psychodynamic explanations of suicide theory did not move too
much from the time of Freud to that of Karl Menninger. In his
important book *Man Against Himself* (1938), Menninger (in capti-
vating ordinary language) delineates the psychodynamics of hostility and asserts that the hostile drive in suicide is made up of three
skeins: (1) the wish to kill, (2) the wish to be killed, and (3) the wish
to die. Gregory Zilboorg refined this psychoanalytic hypothesis
and stated that every suicidal case contained strong, unconscious
hostility combined with an unusual lack of capacity to love others.
He extended the concern from solely intrapsychic dynamics to the
external world and maintained that the role of a broken home in
suicidal proneness demonstrated that suicide has both intrapsychic and external etiological elements.

In addition to the sociological and psychological approaches to the study of suicide, there is a third main contemporary thrust that might be called the philosophical or existential. Albert Camus, in his essay *The Myth of Sisyphus*, begins by saying: "There is but one serious philosophic problem and that is suicide." The principal task of man is to respond to life's apparent meaninglessness despair, and its absurd quality. Ludwig Wittgenstein also states that the main ethical issue for man is suicide. To Camus, Wittgenstein, and other philosophers, however, their ruminations were never meant as prescriptions for action. Arthur Schopenhauer (1788-1860), the philosopher of pessimism, lived to a fairly ripe age and died of natural causes.

Psychological Characteristics of Suicide

Suicide has been related to many emotions: hostility, despair, shame, guilt, dependency, hopelessness, ennui. The traditional psychoanalytic position, first stated by Wilhelm Stekel at a meeting in Vienna in 1910, is that "No one kills himself who has not wanted to kill another or at least wished the death of another." This thought became translated into the psychoanalytic formulation that suicide represented hostility toward the introjected (ambivalently identified) love object. Currently, even psychodynamically oriented suicidologists believe that although hostility can be an important psychological component in some suicides, other emotional states—especially frustrated dependency and hopelessness and helplessness—often play the dominant role in the psychological drama of suicide. If there is one general psychological state commonly assumed to be associated with suicide it is a state of intolerable emotion (or unbearable or "unrepeatable despair")—what Herman Melville, in his masterpiece on self-destruction, *Moby Dick*, called "insufferable anguish."

Over and above the emotional states related to suicide, there are three important general psychological characteristics of suicide:

(1) The first is that the acute suicidal crisis (or period of high and dangerous lethality) is an interval of relatively short duration—to be counted, typically, in hours or days, not usually in months or years. An individual is at a peak of self-destructiveness for a brief time and is either helped, cools off, or is dead. Although one can live for years at a chronically elevated self-destructive level, one cannot have a loaded gun to one's head for too long before either bullet or emotion is discharged.

(2) The second concept is ambivalence. Few persons now dispute that Freud's major insights relating to the role of unconscious motivation (and the workings of what is called the unconscious mind) have been one of the giant concepts of this century in revolutionizing our view of man. The notion of ambivalence is a critical concept in 20th-century, psychodynamically-oriented psychiatry and psychology. The dualities, complications, concomitant contradictory feelings, attitudes, and thrusts toward essentially the same person or introjected image are recognized hallmarks of psychological life. The dualities of the mind's flow constitute a cardinal feature of man's inner life. One can no longer ask in a simple Aristotelian way, "Make up your mind." To such a question a sophisticated respondent ought to say: "But that is precisely the point. I am at least of two, perhaps several, minds on this subject." A law has equal force whether it is passed in the Senate by a 100-0 or a 51-49 vote; so has a bullet. The paradigm of suicide is not the simplistic one of wanting to or not wanting to. The prototypical psychological picture of a person on the brink of suicide is one who wants to and does not want to. He makes plans for self-destruction and at the same time entertains fantasies of rescue and intervention. It is possible—indeed probably prototypical—for a suicidal individual to cut his throat and to cry for help at the same time.

(3) Most suicidal events are dyadic events, that is, two-person events. Actually this dyadic aspect of suicide has two phases: the first during the prevention of suicide when one must deal with the "significant other," and the second in the aftermath in the case of a committed suicide in which one must deal with the survivor-victim. Although it is obvious that the suicidal drama takes place within an individual's head, it is also true that most suicidal tensions are between two people keenly known to each other: spouse, parent and child, lover and lover. In addition, death itself is an extremely dyadic event.

The cold sociological truth is that some modes of death are more stigmatizing to the survivors than are other modes of death and that, generally speaking, suicide imposes the greatest stigma of all upon its survivors. The British physician John Hinton deals with this in his book *Dying* (1967). Hinton also comments that the notes left by the suicidal subject often cause further anguish.

Suicide notes provide an unusual window into the thoughts and feelings of a suicidal person. Various surveys in different places indicate that about 15% of individuals who commit suicide leave suicide notes—although the actual range is from 2 to 30%. By the

1970s fewer than 20 systematic studies of suicide notes had been completed. One of the first scientific studies of suicide notes was by W. Morgenthaler (1945) in a monograph that reported 47 suicide notes (in German) from Bern, Switz. The best-known reports in the United States are by Edwin S. Shneidman and Norman L. Farberow (1947, 1970) in their studies of genuine suicide notes and elicited matched notes written by nonsuicidal persons. Suicide notes have been subjected to a number of types of analyses: by emotional states, logical styles, "reasons" stated or implied, death wishes, language characteristics, relations to persons, and by computer count of key "tag words." In general these analyses indicate that (1) it is possible to distinguish between genuine and simulated suicide notes, and, more importantly, (2) genuine suicide notes are characterized by dichotomous logic, greater amount of hostility and self-blame, use of very specific names and instructions to the survivor, more decisiveness, less evidence of thinking about thinking, and more use of the various meanings of the word "love."

The Two Fundamental Aspects of Death and Suicide

Twentieth-century philosophers, especially Percy Bridgman (1938), pointed out that there is an epistemological characteristic unique to death, specifically that there are two fundamental aspects of death: the private aspect, as an individual lives it himself (my dying); and the public aspect, as one can experience, in reality, the death of another (your death). In death (and suicide) there is a key difference between the principal actor and the observer. One major implication of this key difference is that I can observe and experience your death (just as you can observe and experience my death), but I can never experience my own death for if I could, I should still be alive.

Some of this kind of thinking operates in suicide, especially when it is seen as a psychological magical act. Just as Melville wrote that "All evil, to crazy Ahab, were visibly personified and made practically assailable in Moby Dick," so to the suicidal mind, using this same tortured logic, the whole world is "made practically assailable" and can be thought to be expunged by destroying oneself.

The fantasies of one's own suicide can represent the greatest possible combination of omnipotence and potential realization of effectiveness—greater even than one's fantasies of the assassination of another, group revenge, mass murder, or even genocide. Any "average" individual can say: "From my point of view, suicide destroys all"—and it can be done.

These inferred psychodynamics of suicide (relating to delusions of annihilation) are thought by psychoanalysts to have their origins in the earliest notions of an individual's infantile omnipotence. The literature of suicide in Western man, however, continually emphasizes that suicide can be an individual's final act, his final escape hatch, his final revenge—often misconstrued as a final 'right." This unique epistemological dual characteristic of death (the difference between my dying and your death) is fundamental to an understanding of suicide.

Attempted Suicide

Although it is obvious that one has to "attempt" suicide in order to commit it, it is equally clear that often the event of "attempting suicide" does not have death (cessation) as its objective. It is an acknowledged fact that often the goal of "attempted suicide" (such as cutting oneself or ingesting harmful substances) is to change one's life (or to change the "significant others" around one) rather than to end it. On the other hand, sometimes death is intended and only fortuitously avoided. After that, one's life—what has been called "a bonus life"—is forever somewhat different. Alfred Alvarez, who himself made a serious suicide attempt, said that survivors have a changed life, with entirely different standards.

Erwin Stengel, a student of attempted suicide, in his arguments and statistical presentations, seems to suggest, in the main, that persons who attempt suicide and those who commit suicide represent essentially two different "populations"—with admittedly some overflow from the first to the second. It is useful to think of two sets of overlapping populations: (1) a group of those who attempt suicide, few of whom go on to commit it, and (2) a group of those who commit suicide, many of whom have previously attempted it. A great deal has to do with the lethality of the event. Lethality is roughly synonymous with the "deathfulness" of the act and is an important dimension in understanding any potentially suicidal person. Avery D. Weisman in 1972 distinguished three aspects of lethality: that of intention (ideation and involvement); that of implementation (risk and rescue); and that of intercession (resources, relief, and reorientation). The ratio between suicide attempts and commits is about 8 to 1—1 committed suicide for every 8 attempts.

Suicide attempts have many meanings and, whatever their level of lethality, ought to be taken seriously. A person who attempts suicide because he believes that there is no use living may not necessarily mean that he wants to die but that he has exhausted the potential for being someone who matters.

Partial Death and Substitutes for Suicide

Sometimes the very life-style of an individual seems to truncate and demean his life so that he is as good as dead. Often alcoholism, drug addiction, mismanagement of physical disease (such as diabetes or Buerger's disease), and masochistic behaviour can be seen in this light. A study of gifted individuals (with IQ's over 140) indicated that conspicuous failure in adult life—a kind of "partial death"—was sometimes the "price" for life as a substitute for overt suicide.

The chief theorist of the concept of partial death is Karl Menninger. Much of his conception is explicated in *Man Against Himself*. Menninger writes of (1) chronic suicide, including asceticism, martyrdom, neurotic invalidism, alcohol addiction, antisocial behavior, and psychosis; (2) focal suicide—focused on a limited part of the body—including self-mutilations, malingering, multiple surgery, purposive accidents, impotence, and frigidity; and (3) organic suicide, focusing on the psychological factors in organic disease, especially the self-punishing, aggressive, and erotic components. In the 1970s, the focus was on concepts such as indirect self-destructive behavior. There has been a large number of studies of alcoholism and drug addiction and diabetes and on aspects of homicide (on both the murderer and the victim) as suicidal equivalents. In relation to the role of the homicidal victim in his own death, the work of Marvin Wolfgang (1958) has been particularly interesting.

A related concept is that of "subintentioned death." That concept asserts that there are many deaths that are neither clearly suicidal nor clearly accidental or natural but are deaths in which the decedent has played some covert or unconscious role in "permitting" his death to occur, sort of "accidentally," or by "inviting" homicide, or, by unconsciously disregarding what could be life-

extending medical regimen, and thus dying sooner than "necessary." Losing the "will to live" and so-called voodoo deaths—as
well as many deaths in ordinary society—can be viewed as sub-
intentional deaths. Obviously, this view of death changes the
nature and statistics of suicide dramatically (Shneidman, 1963).

This concept of a reduced level of life as a substitute (or psychological "trade") for suicide itself presents fascinating philosophic,
social, psychological, and moral questions that relate to whether or
not there actually is an irreducible suicide rate among human
beings. Is there a price for civilization? Indeed, a price for life?
Litman, reflecting on Freud's work, agrees with Freud's general
schematic view and that there is a suicidal trend in everyone. This
self-destructiveness is controlled through constructive habits of
living and loving, but when they break down, the individual may
easily be forced into a suicidal crisis. To keep alive one must keep
his thoughts, feelings, and aspirations in a vital balance.

Suicide and Religion

I n the Western world it has been traditionally said that
the suicide rate is higher among Protestants than among
Catholics or Jews and that the latter group shows significantly low suicidal figures. By the 1970s it was known,
however, that the role of religion in relation to suicide is more
complicated and that religious affiliation serves both to inhibit
and, at other times, to facilitate suicide. At the outset it is important
to distinguish between religious beliefs and religious (social) affiliation. Durkheim not unexpectedly emphasized the sociological
aspects of religion. He stated: "If religion protects one from the
desire for self-destruction, it is not because it preaches to him, with
elements of religious origin, repect for one's person; it is because it
forms a social group." A nationwide study in the United States
indicated that the pro rata suicide rate among veterans—a fairly
representative group of U.S. citizenry—for Catholics and Protestants was about equal to the numbers (and percentages) of Protestants and Catholics in the country generally. Much more important
than nominal religious affiliation would be a number of subtleties
of religious belief: the feeling of group belongingness, belief in an
omnipotent God, belief in the efficacy of prayer, belief in a hereafter
or existence after death, and other issues relating to death in
general. Results of a national U.S. survey of 30,000 persons re-

ported by Shneidman in 1970 indicated that a sizable percentage (57%) of individuals of all religious backgrounds (and with a variety of intensities of religious belief) did not believe in any life after death and that over one-third indicated that religion had played either a relatively minor role or no role at all in the development of their attitudes toward death (and toward suicide). Just as in the 20th century there has been an enormous "secularization" of death—the physician and hospital in many ways replacing the clergyman and the church in relation to the anxieties surrounding death—so too has there been a secularization of suicide. Few of the current debates about suicide are on primary religious grounds; when the ethics of suicide are debated, those usually are in terms of such concepts as "freedom" and "life," *i.e.,* how free an individual should be to take his own life and how far "benign intervention" should go in an attempt to save an individual's life before the intervention is intrusive and robs the person of more than his life is worth.

When Durkheim spoke of religion as a source of social organization (holding individuals together with common beliefs and practices), he was not only speaking of social integration but he was also, from a psychological point of view, referring to personal identification. Walter T. Martin and Jack P. Gibbs (1964) proposed a theory relating status integration with suicide and Henry and Short (1954) discussed the positive relationship between suicide and status and the negative relation between suicide and the strength of a relational source. In general it appears that a person who is uneasy in his religion (or in his irreligion) or changes his religion several times (like a person who is uneasy in his marriage or has several marriages) is more likely to commit suicide, not so much on purely religious (or marital) grounds but because of his general perturbation and lack of good self-concept, which underlie his uneasy search for certainty and stability in his life.

Suicide and the Law

Not surprisingly, the history of suicide and the law closely parallel and reflect—often with significant lags—the major cultural and philosophic attitudes toward suicide. Probably the most important recent legal change was the passage of the Suicide Act in England in 1961 that (1) finally abolished criminal penalties for committing suicide—considering that in the 19th century (as late as 1823), a London citizen who committed suicide was buried at a crossroads in Chelsea with a stake pounded through his heart; (2) no longer made survivors of suicide attempts liable to criminal prosecution; and (3) as a kind of quid pro quo for the liberalization of the first two measures, increased the penalties (up to 14 years' imprisonment) for aiding and abetting a suicidal act. Earlier, the Homicide Act of 1957 changed the charge against a survivor of a suicide pact from murder to manslaughter.

In the United States, most aspects of suicide are not against the law. As of the early 1970s a comparatively small number of states (9) listed suicide as a crime, although no penalties (such as mutilation of bodies or forfeiture of estates) were exacted. In such states suicide attempts are either felonies or misdemeanors and could result in jail sentences, although such laws are selectively or indifferently enforced. Two states (Nevada and New York) repealed such laws, stating in effect that although suicide is "a grave social wrong" there is no way to punish it. Eighteen states—Alaska, Arkansas, California, Florida, Kansas, Louisiana, Michigan, Massachusetts, Minnesota, Mississippi, Missouri, Montana, Nevada, New Mexico, New York, Oregon, Wisconsin, and Wyoming— have no laws against either suicide or suicide attempts but specify that to aid, advise, or encourage another person to commit suicide is a felony. In the more than 20 other states, that are no penal statutes referring to suicide.

In the early 1970s, especially in Great Britain, there was some movement (among some eminent lawyers, theologians, philosophers, and physicians) toward the legalization of voluntary euthanasia; proposals were to repeal the aiding and abetting aspect of suicide laws so that a physician might, on a patient's request, assist him to his own voluntary death.

Some Oddities of Suicide

The lore about suicide contains a large number of interesting and esoteric items about various cultures. Suicide was thought, for example, to be absent among so-called primitive cultures, but it is evident that this is not so. Studies were made of suicide in Africa (Paul Bohannan, 1960), India (Verrier Elwin, 1943; Upendra Thakur, 1963), Hong Kong (Yap Powmeng, 1958), and Japan (Ohara, 1961). Practically every popular article on suicide routinely contains a statement about the kamikaze pilots who flew and died for Japan in World War II. Also, in relation to Japan, one often reads of the practice of a hara-kiri or seppuku, which is the ritual act of disemboweling oneself and was limited to the samurai warrior and noble classes. General Tōjō, who attempted hara-kiri at the end of World War II, was saved by U.S. doctors, only to be hanged later by a military tribunal. In 1970 the widely-known Japanese novelist Mishima Yukio committed sep-puku (with ritual self-disemboweling and decapitation) at the age of 45. In general, however, suicide in contemporary Japan is more "Western" than otherwise—often done with barbiturates. In a discussion of suicide in 19th-century India one finds references to suttee, the custom in which Hindu widows threw themselves onto the funeral pyres of their husbands.

Six suicides are recorded in the Old Testament: Abimelech, Samson, Saul, Saul's armour bearer, Ahithophel, and Zimri. The most famous and among the most frequently cited suicides per-haps, are Socrates' drinking hemlock and Cato's throwing himself upon his sword. The apocryphal stories of Bismarck's contemplat-ing suicide, Napoleon's attempting suicide, Washington's despon-dency, and Lincoln's depression keep reappearing in articles on suicide—including this one.

Myths of Suicide

Following is a summary of some of the more outstanding miscon-ceptions of suicide:

Fable: Persons who talk about suicide do not commit suicide. *Fact:* Of any ten persons who will themselves commit it, eight have given definite warnings of their suicidal intentions.

Fable: Suicide happens without warning. *Fact:* Studies reveal that the suicidal person gives many clues and warnings regarding his suicidal intentions.

Fable: Suicidal persons are fully intent on dying. *Fact:* Most suicidal persons are undecided about living or dying, and they "gamble with death," leaving it to others to save them. Almost no one commits suicide without letting others know how he is feeling.

Fable: Once a person is suicidal, he is suicidal forever. *Fact:* Individuals who wish to kill themselves are suicidal only for a limited period of time.

Fable: Improvement following a suicidal crisis means that the suicidal risk is over. *Fact:* Most suicides occur within about three months following the beginning of "improvement," when the individual has the energy to put his morbid thoughts and feelings into effect.

Fable: Suicide strikes much more often among the rich, or, conversely, it occurs almost exclusively among the poor. *Fact:* Suicide is neither the rich man's disease nor the poor man's curse. Suicide is represented proportionately among all levels of society.

Fable: Suicide is inherited or "runs in the family." *Fact:* It follows individual patterns.

Fable: All suicidal individuals are mentally ill, and suicide always is the act of a psychotic person. *Fact:* Studies of hundreds of genuine suicide notes indicate that although the suicidal person is extremely unhappy, he is not necessarily mentally ill.

Romantic Suicide and the Artist

Since at least the 16th century, specifically in the Italian commedia dell'arte, there has been a character named Harlequin who typically wears a multi-colored suit and a black mask—and has a connection with death. Indeed to be loved by Harlequin was to be married to death. This is the idea of death as a lover; it relates to the romanticization of death itself. As a refinement of this idea, suicide has historically been thought to be a romantic kind of death. One specific myth is that suicide is caused by unrequited love. Suicide pacts (portrayed romantically in *Mayerling* and in *Elvira Madigan*) are depicted as the essence of intense love. One result of this mystique is a belief that especially sensitive people, artists—poets, painters, and writers—are unusually prone to commit suicide and, indeed, add to their reputations as artists by committing suicide. Perhaps the best-known novel of this genre is Goethe's *The Sorrows of Young Werther,* published in 1774 when the author was 24 years old and credited, in the mythology of suicide, with having created a veritable epidemic of romantic suicides throughout Europe. By the 1970s the list of suicides of artists was sufficiently long and vivid to persuade an uncritical student of suicide that the sensitivity of the artist is somehow related to the special nature of a romantic suicidal death. The list includes Van Gogh, Virginia Woolf, Hart Crane, the Italian writer Cesare Pavese, Randall Jarrell, Modigliani, Jackson Pollock, Mark Rothko, Ernest Hemingway, John Berryman, Sylvia Plath, Mishima, and Kawabata Yasunari. Perhaps the best description and analysis of suicide and the creative literary artist is by the English poetry editor and critic

Alfred Alvarez in his book *The Savage God: a Study of Suicide* (1971). Maksim Gorki attempted suicide when he was 19. One of the most romanticized suicides in Western literature is that of the English poet Thomas Chatterton (1752-70), who took poison at the age of 17. This particular death illustrates the notion (or myth) "that those with more life and passion go soon"—that the best die young. It reminds one of those who have died "too young"—Byron, Shelley, Keats, Mozart—and the particular poignancy of an untimely death of an especially beautiful or gifted person. We tend to be essentially undemocratic about death and suicide—because we tend to believe that some deaths level (or elevate) certain people more than others.

Statistics on Suicide

T he demographic use of statistics on suicide perhaps were given their greatest impetus by John Graunt and Johann Peter Süssmilch. Graunt was a London tradesman who, in 1662, published a small book of observations on the London bills of mortality. He separated various bits of information contained in these rolls of names of the dead into separate categories and organized the information systematically, finally constructing mortality tables—the first attempt to organize data in that manner. Of great significance was his success in demonstrating the regularities that can be found between medical and social phenomena when one deals with large numbers. He demonstrated how an analysis of the mortality statistics could be used to the advantage of physicians, businessmen, and government.

Much of what is known today as statistical information came into existence with the work of Süssmilch, a Prussian clergyman who in 1741 in his analyses of vital data from church registers created political arithmetic, or what is now called vital statistics. It is important to keep in mind that statistics, particularly statistics on suicide, are in part socially manufactured data—mostly by coroners and physicians. Suicidal deaths are notoriously underrepresented and obviously vary from country to country dependent not only on the number of suicides that in fact occur in each country but also on deeply ingrained cultural folkways relating to the social, cultural, and religious attitudes of that country.

There are several sources of suicide statistics. Louis Dublin's text, *Suicide* (1963), is a standard source; the World Health Organization (WHO) booklet, *The Prevention of Suicide* (1968), is another. *Suicide in the United States, 1950-1964* (1967) and *The Facts of Life and Death* (1970), both published by the U.S. Department of Health, Education, and Welfare, are standard sources in the United States. In general, the reported suicide rate for the United States is between 10 and 12 per 100,000, which places the United States about in the middle of the countries that report to the United Nations. Austria, West Germany, Hungary, Japan, Czechoslovakia, Denmark, Finland, Sweden, and Switzerland report rates of over 25 per 100,000 population, and Italy, the Netherlands, and Spain report rates under 10 per 100,000. The number of suicides in the United States per year is given at about 22,000 but many experts believe the actual number to be at least twice as high.

In any discussion of the statistics of suicide—keeping in mind their tenuous character—it is important to distinguish among rank, rate, and number. Currently, in the United States, suicide is ranked among the first five causes of death for white males from 10 to 55. For example, suicide is the second-ranked cause of death for white males age 15-19, but one must appreciate that the first leading cause of death, accidents, yields 627 chances in 100,000 of the individual's dying from that cause, while suicide yields (only) 88 chances in 100,000. Generally, in the early ages when suicide is high, it occupies that rank because the other killers like heart disease, malignant neoplasms (cancer), vascular lesions of the central nervous system (stroke), and cirrhosis of the liver are not then common.

In general, statistics on suicide in the 19th and 20th centuries indicate that more men than women commit suicide (about 3 to 1) and that more women than men attempt suicide (again about 3 to 1). In the early 1970s there was evidence that the ratio for committed suicide seemed to be changing, moving toward (but not yet achieving) an equal proportion between the sexes. Statistics relating to race and ethnic origin seem to be undergoing changes, probably reflecting general changes in attitude toward the concept of race and ethnicity. In the United States it was reported for years that Caucasian suicides far outnumbered Black suicides, but the rate for Blacks seems to be changing, moving closer to that for Caucasians. Whether this reflects the effects of urban ghetto living, the effects of identifying with "the white man's problems," or simply better and more accurate record-keeping are all issues for further study. Some studies (conducted in England and Australia) that followed individuals who emigrated either to the United States or to Australia seem to indicate that the suicide rates of specific groups such as Hungarians, Italians, Poles, and Irish appear, for a generation or so, to be closer to the rates of the homeland than to the rates of the adopted country. In these data, there are many methodological issues left to be resolved.

In relation to suicide statistics, a standard textbook on sociology published in 1972 reported that sociologists still made continuous reference to the work of Durkheim. Rates derived from Durkheim's studies show that suicide rates for Protestants have been consistently higher than those for Jews or Catholics. In the early part of the 20th century the Jewish rate in the Netherlands was higher than the Protestant, and during the depression, in Toronto, Can., Catholic rates also were higher than Protestant. The inference is that the time, the place, and the social circumstances are all important factors.

In the matter of comparative national statistics, Alvarez points out that U.S. Pres. Dwight D. Eisenhower blamed the high Swedish suicide rate on what too much social welfare can do. But the present rate in Sweden, Alvarez notes, is about the same as it was in 1910, before comprehensive social welfare programs were begun and is actually ranked ninth on a table published by WHO. The countries of Central Europe show the highest rates: Hungary has the highest national rate; Austria and Czechoslovakia are third and fourth. The highest suicide rate in the world is that of West Berlin; its rate is more than twice that of West Germany as a whole. The city, it has been suggested, is a model of what Durkheim called anomie—alienated not only geographically but also in cultural, social, and political aspects. Countries like Ireland and Egypt, where suicide is considered by many a mortal sin, have rates among the lowest in the world, bearing out Stengel's conclusion that highly industrialized and prosperous countries tend to have comparatively high suicide rates. Alvarez concludes that official statistics reflect only a fraction of the true figures, which a number of authorities reckon to be anywhere from a quarter to a half again as large. Because of religious and bureaucratic prejudices, family sensitivity, differences in the proceedings of coroners' hearings and postmortem examinations, the shadowy distinctions between suicides and accidents—in short, the unwillingness to recognize the act for what it is—knowledge of the extent to which suicide pervades modern society is diminished and distorted.

A certain sizable percentage of deaths that are certified by coroners or medical examiners—estimated to be between 10 and

15%—are equivocal as to what the actual mode of death ought to be; this uncertainty usually lies between suicide or accident. A procedure, called the psychological autopsy, has been developed to deal with these equivocal deaths. Essentially, the psychological autopsy involves the use of social and behavioral scientists (psychologists, psychiatrists, social workers, and other trained personnel) who interview relatives and friends of the decedent with the goal of developing information about the decedent's intention vis-á-vis his own death in the days just before the death. Clues—verbal ("You won't be seeing me around"); behavioral (giving away prized possessions or marked changes in patterns of eating, sexuality, interests); or situational (the loss of a loved one)—are deemed to point more to suicide than to accident. In the absence of such clues, a recommendation for a non-suicidal or "undetermined" mode of death should be made to the certifying official.

Suicide Vention (Prevention, Intervention, Postvention)

The Latin word *venire* means "to come" or "to do." In relation to any event (*e.g.,* suicide) one can act before, during, or after—corresponding to prevention, intervention, and postvention. These terms also correspond roughly to the public health concepts of primary, secondary, and tertiary prevention.

Prevention

If, as this article has suggested, suicidal phenomena are existential-social-psychological-dyadic events, then obviously primary prevention is enormously complicated—almost tantamount to preventing human unhappiness. Some students of human nature believe that the urge toward self-destruction is ubiquitous and that a certain amount of it is an inevitable and constant price of civilization, if not of life itself. Primarily, prevention would relate to the principles of good mental hygiene in general.

Intervention

Intervention relates to the treatment and care of suicidal crisis or suicidal problems. On this score, suicide prevention centers could be more accurately labeled suicide intervention centers. A great deal has been learned about practical techniques for effective suicide intervention. There is a vast literature on therapy and treatment of suicidal persons in various settings—in the community, in suicide prevention and crisis intervention centers, in poison-control centers, in outpatient offices, and in both medical and mental hospitals. In general, most of the suggestions for care have in common the stressing of good rapport, working with the "significant others" in the suicidal person's life, using the available community resources for referral (for emotional support, legal aid, financial help, employment, individual and group psychotherapy, hospitalization), and focusing on the reduction of the person's "lethality" during the period of suicidal crisis. Much of the suicide prevention work borrows from the theory of crisis intervention developed by Erich Lindemann (1944) and Gerald Caplan (1964). In the United States, the theoretical and empirical work of the Los Angeles Suicide Prevention Center, established in 1955, and in Great Britain, the work of the Samaritans, established in 1953, has been widely emulated.

In 1960 there were fewer than a half-dozen suicide prevention centers in the United States; a decade later there were over 200. Typically they are telephone-answering centers; maintaining 24-hour service, they serve as short-term resources, are theoretically modeled in terms of the concept of crisis intervention, and use both professional and lay volunteer staff.

Suicide is best understood as a socio-psychological, existential human event that calls for compassionate response to an individual in an emotional and philosophic crisis. Obviously suicide is not solely a medical problem and many kinds of persons including volunteers—provided they are carefully selected, well-trained, and continuously supervised—can serve as lifesaving agents in the prevention of suicide. The lay volunteer has been described as probably the most important single discovery in the history of suicide prevention. Nonetheless, professionally trained persons—psychologists, psychiatrists, social workers—continue to play the primary roles in suicide prevention and especially in research.

Postvention

A term introduced by Shneidman in 1971, refers to those things done after the dire event has occurred that serve to mollify the aftereffects of the event in a person who has attempted suicide, or to deal with the adverse effects on the survivor-victims of a person who has committed suicide. It is offering psychological services to the bereaved survivors. It includes work with the surviving children, parents, and spouses. Much of postventive work has been focused on widows. Studies show that survivors are apt to have a higher morbidity and mortality rate in the year following the death of their loved one than comparable persons who are not survivors of such a death. It may well be that the major public mental-health challenge in suicide lies in offering postventive help to the survivor-victims. The development of postvention is part of the current new view of the special psychological needs relating to death.

A Psychological Theory of Suicide

T he purpose of this paper is to advance and illustrate a theoretical formulation relating to the psychological components of suicidal behavior.

Before I turn to any formulation of the psychological ingredients of a suicidal act, I should state that what is being discussed here is one specific kind of suicidal deed, the rather suddenly executed suicidal act. This kind of suicidal behavior has, in general, the following characteristics:

1. it is calculated by the suicidal person to be fatal, and it usually entails jumping, shooting, burning, or hanging;
2. it is decided upon rather suddenly, a few days or even just minutes before the event; and
3. it is not directly communicated to others. Indirect "cries for help," arising from the omnipresent ambivalence that exists until the moment of a fatal act, are made, but these are either disregarded or not heard by potential rescuers.

Like an explosion, an unexpected suicide is a combination of three main ingredients and the presence of an igniting spark. Dynamite consists essentially of nitroglycerin, saltpeter, and a carbonaceous material such as charcoal; the explosion is sparked by the application of heat. In a somewhat analogous way, a sudden suicidal act has three main components and requires one igniting process. These four elements of suicide are:

1. Heightened inimicality.
2. Exacerbation of perturbation.
3. Increased constriction of intellectual focus; tunneling or narrowing of the mind's content.
4. The idea of cessation: the insight that it is possible to stop consciousness and put an end to suffering. This is the igniting element that explodes the mixture.

From *Psychiatric Annals*, Nov., 1976, Vol. 6, No. 11, pp. 51-66, inclusive. Reprinted with permission of Insight Publishing Company.

Let us examine each of these elements.

Inimicality

The word comes from *amicus*, friend, and the prefix *in*, meaning not. So *inimicality* refers to those qualities within the individual that are unfriendly towards the self—specifically, the ways in which he is his own worst enemy. We can totally avoid any notion of a death instinct and still see as a matter of common knowledge that an ordinary person, complicated as he is and living with a variety of goals and urges that are often contradictory to each other, occasionally has to work at cross-purposes within his psyche. All of us have psychodynamic histories relating to parental figures; consequently we have ways of succeeding and failing in which we do things that are clearly not in our own best interests. These relate to many aspects of our lives: matters of diet, smoking, conduct with our peers and our superiors, our work habits, our patterns of success and failure, etc. No closely examined life fails to reveal its fair quota of inimical threads.

It is possible to evaluate the inimicality "thrust" in a person on a numerical scale. Actually, two scales might be used: one to rate the person's modal or characterologic inimicality for his or her time of life and the other to rate inimicality as it exists at any particular moment. Usually the two are the same, but obviously acute exacerbations of the inimicality thrust can occur within one person over and above the modal level. The suicidal state occurs in a person with heightened inimicality, performing acts against his or her best interests at a level higher than the modal. The life is not going well in terms of felt pressures (physical health, rejection, inner feelings of failure, pain, whatever), and the subject is not handling those pressures and feelings to the best of his or her abilities. Minute indices of loss or failure indicate the heightened inimicality, almost in the way that petechiae can be the dermal hallmarks of inner disease.

The conceptual relationship between inimicality and masochism would seem *a priori* to be close. The intrapsychic modality of masochism is punishment, and in Litman's words, "In order to provoke punishment the masochist must do what is inexpedient, must act against his own interests, must ruin his prospects, and perhaps destroy himself." (The traditional psychoanalytic argument relating to the death instinct need not concern us here.) I would prefer that the concepts of inimicality and masochism not be thought of as coterminous or isomorphic but that inimicality be viewed as a broader and not necessarily pathologic thread in each person's psychologic makeup. It is quite different from "malignant masochism," where there seems to be superego pathology and often an incorporated parent figure that is seen as demanding death in order to obtain love.

Whereas malignant masochism is an infrequent clinical finding, I believe that inimicality (or general masochism) is omnipresent and that the highly suicidal condition contains a state of heightened inimicality. This may appear to some as a tautology: self-destructive (suicidal) people are inimical (self-destructive). Nevertheless, in order to assess an acute suicidal state one would be on the lookout for elements of heightened general self-destructiveness.

Perturbation

Perturbation refers to how disturbed, "shook up," ill at ease, or mentally upset a person is. It ranges from total silent withdrawal or hyperactive violence, at the far end of the scale, to equanimity and peace of mind, on the near end. Everyone is ratable on two scales of perturbation, both the characterologically typical level for that person and his or her perturbation state at the moment. The suicidal state always involves some heightened inner turmoil, with an acute, passionate debate within the confines of the mind. The person, at least inwardly and usually outwardly also, is in a state of heightened perturbation; he is disturbed, anxious, perhaps depressed or agitated, but certainly not at his most equanimous. The combination of heightened inimicality and heightened perturbation begins the necessary mixture of a potentially suicidal state.

Admittedly, perturbation is difficult to define. In a sense, it encompasses all psychiatric nomenclature and terminology. But in the same way that we have established such concepts as "free-floating anxiety," we need a term that cuts across and includes all the A.P.A. categories of psychic dysfunctioning and mental "disease" in order to express general upset. There are dangers in trying to be too specific—especially in trying to tie all suicide to depression, which is only one form of perturbation. But this much seems clear enough: heightened perturbation is a universal, although not sufficient, concomitant of the suicidal act.

Perturbation, by definition, involves negative emotional states rather than positive ones. Henry A. Murray, combining some published experimental work from VA hospitals with his analysis of Melville's works, has proposed five negative emotional states that he found most characteristic both of Melville's writings of and men who committed suicide in VA hospitals. These are (1) pitiful forlornness, deprivation, distress, and grief; (2) extrapunitiveness (blaming others), anger, hate, and physical aggressiveness; (3) intrapunitiveness, remorse, guilt, depression, and need for punishment; (4) egression (leaving the scene) and desertion; and (5) affectlessness, which is one variety of being "dead to the world," an equivalent to mute withdrawal that includes disgust, bitterness, and sardonic humor. The reader is encouraged to read Murray's full account of these psychological states in *Essays in Self-Destruction* (1967).

Constriction

The concept of constriction is an old one in psychiatry and psychology, and Erwin Ringel and others have mentioned it in relation to suicide. It is sometimes metaphorically called the tunneling of vision, a narrowing of the mind's eye.* Boris Pasternak, in discussing the suicides of a number of young Russian poets, described this concept as a constriction of memory and associations that would ordinarily occur to the mind. One's ordinary thoughts and loves and feelings and responsibilities are simply not available to the consciousness. One does not "forget" that he is married; rather, the tie to the spouse is suddenly blocked out and disappears. The suicidal person turns his back on the past and permits his memories to become unreal; thus they cannot serve to save him. In this tunneled vision, the focus is on the unbearable emotion and on the ways to escape from it.

An important characteristic of constriction is the role of dichotomous thinking (Neuringer, 1976). The suicidal person abandons the

---

*On second reflection, perhaps this condition ought more accurately be called "stope vision" rather than "tunnel vision." A tunnel—even a "tunnel of extended pain"—always, by definition, has an opening—freedom, air, light, release—at its other end; a stope—a term used in mining—is an underground excavation in which miners perform their work; it is often a cul-de-sac, a "dead end" with no exit except the way that one came in. (But we cannot reverse *time* and come out of any temporal sequence at the same moment that we entered). The suicidal person confuses a stope with a tunnel. Most dire, baleful, painful situations—excepts perhaps some terminal illnesses—are "merely" tunnels; the constricted mind sees these transient passages as permanent stopes. It is hard for me to resist using the phrase that suicide is the stoping of consciousness.

sense of life's continuum and uses such words as "only," "either/or," "always," "never," and "forever." In the example that follows, the young woman who jumped from a high balcony said that the "only" thing she could do was to lose consciousness and the "only" way to lose consciousness was to jump from something "good and high"—statements that, taken in the world at large, are manifestly ridiculous. But when the mind constricts, the anguished person sees only the mechanism for solving the problems within the context of increased inimicality and perturbation.

When this unhappy triad of heightened inimicality, elevated perturbation, and increasing constriction exists, the subject is then incipiently suicidal. The concept of lethality, which relates to the probability of the subject's killing himself, means precisely that these three components are actively present.

Cessation

The spark that ignites this potentially explosive mixture is the idea that one can put a stop to the pain. The idea of cessation (death, stopping, or eternal sleep) provides the solution for the desperate person. It permits him or her to resolve the unbearable state of self-destructiveness, disturbance, and isolation. In an inimical, perturbed, constricted person, once that idea crosses into consciousness, the suicidal act has begun. The idea of cessation— that I can be out of it, that I can handle the situation, that I can solve this mess, pay off my debts, take revenge, release myself from anguish, stop the process of the cancer—is the turning point in the suicidal drama.

What is especially tragic is that this idea of cessation is often not communicated by suicidal persons. For example, a therapist is often well aware of heightened inimicality and perturbation, and he may be listening to the patient's dichotomous thinking. But the idea of cessation, because it is so dramatic and so breathtaking and so dangerous, is often kept a secret from the therapist. It follows from this that any talk of committing suicide must be investigated very carefully and very seriously. Talk of being dead, of going away, of ending it all (especially in the presence of the three other factors) should alert one to a highly lethal suicidal state.

The assessment of suicidality can be conceived as a profile of these four factors. The suicidal state is one in which all four factors are above a certain threshold of dangerousness. The route to suicide prevention is not in disputing about the beguilements of cessation but in working vigorously to reduce the inimicality and perturbation in the patient. Clinically, it would appear that perturbation is the most amenable to first-order treatment by reassurance; by fostering the transference relationship through being a strong, dependable, benign figure in the patient's life; by helping the patient in practical ways; or by the adjunctive use of chemotherapy.

In all of this, the lines of communication should be kept open, and the suicidal person needs to understand that his or her sufferings are appreciated. In this way, the therapist and patient can work mutually on reducing the components that make up the suicidal act.

A Case Example

The following is a segment of an interchange between the author and a 30-year-old woman patient. She had attempted suicide during the previous week by ingesting a considerable quantity of secobarbital (Seconal®) and chlorpromazine (Thorazine®) and then, two days later, while in the hospital to which she had been taken, made a more serious attempt by jumping from a fifth-floor balcony. Comments relating to the four psychologic components of suicide are juxtaposed with the verbatim record. The segment, which occurred during the fourth extended interchange between us, was preceded by a few minutes of light, casual talk. With my question "What brings you into the hospital?", I turned the exchange to more serious matters.

Interchange	Comments
S: What brings you into the hospital? What happened to you, and why are you in this bed? T: [Pause.] Well, I had taken an overdose of Seconal [pause], 100 mg. tablets, capsules. I must've taken about 50 of them, plus about 50 tablets of Thorazine. It was about 25 mg. Well, that is, I don't know how lethal that is, but I know Seconal is pretty damn lethal, and	*The incident being discussed here is not the suddenly executed act of immediate lethality. In the "middle range"—lethality suicidal acts such as this one, there is heightened ambivalence (see the note below) and a more prominent role of a discernible precipitating event.*

um ... [pause] I decided I was
gonna go, go off in the woods
somewhere and just lie down and
crump out. [Pause.] So that's what I
did. And once I had taken the pills, I
decided I just couldn't go through
with it—that I really didn't want to
die, that I wanted help. So I walked
back to my apartment, and just as I
got to the door of the building I
collapsed, and I don't remember
very much after that except
apparently someone found me.
S: You don't know who?
T: Yes, I do know who it was—the
wife of the manager of the building,
and I guess she called the
ambulance and I was taken here.
S: What was that event about? Why
did you ingest all that stuff?
T: 'Cause I just ... I had run into a
box that I couldn't get out of—sort
of frantic kind of mental state
which I knew was leading to
something very serious and, um—
you know—possibly hospitalization
of some sort. And I was terribly
confused and disoriented.
S: Had you attempted suicide
before?
T: Yes, but not seriously. Never
with an intent to die. Just with
intent to, I guess, to shake people
up.
S: Just to shake them up? Do you
think what you did that day was
with the intent to die?
T: Uh-huh.
S: But you changed your mind?
T: Yes.
S: Who figured in this?
T: My husband.
S: Your husband? What was the
figuring? What were the feelings
and emotions between you and him
and in your own mind as you
ingested all these pills?
T: Well, it wasn't while I took them;
it was afterwards. I just thought
that I couldn't do it—I just couldn't
do it—because of him.

*There is ambivalence in every
suicidal deed. The debate within
"the congress of the mind" is the
hallmark of the suicidal state. The
suicidal person wishes to die and
concomitantly has fantasies of
rescue and intervention.*

*These words betoken heightened
perturbation, especially the word
"frantic," coupled with the fear of
losing one's mind.*

*A previous suicide attempt ranks
high among the prodromal clues to
a lethal suicidal event.*

*The husband is ambivalently seen.
He is both part of the survival
fantasy and an important element
in the causative nexus. But we also
see the presence of constriction—
"Everyone was very outside ...
of what was going on in my mind."*

S: Was he some part in the motivation of your doing it in the first place?
T: Well, quite possibly he was, but he just seemed not be be. He seemed to be very outside of everything that was going on in my mind. In fact, everyone was very outside.
S: Were there other figures who played a more important role?
T: Not that I was aware of. I was pretty isolated at that point.
S: Had you been sort of spiraling downward for some time?
T: No, not for some time. Well, yes, the ... precisely at the moment of my 30th birthday. [Pause]. I had sort of went into a kind of a panic.
S: That was a big thing—no longer being 20?
T: [Sigh.] Uh-huh ...
S: Yes.
T: Things sort of just got worse and worse.
S: Then what happened?
T: I gather I was brought to the hospital. I guess to the emergency room. And I snuck a look at my chart one day, which I shouldn't have done, and discovered that I guess [pause] the stomach was washed out, or something like that.
S: Let's stop with interesting goodies that you mention. How did you get to look at your chart?
T: They left it, when they took me to x-ray, and left it on my bed.
S: Of course. Okay, please go ahead.
T: Um ... And when I woke up—I don't remember that very too clearly—but when I woke up, I was in a hospital room. No, I remember struggling. They had my wrists in restraints, and I didn't believe that I had done it. I didn't believe that I was ... I knew I was in the hospital, and I realized vaguely that I had taken pills and somehow I had gotten to the hospital.

The isolation and the desperation that accompanies it are evident here.

More description of panic-perturbation, revolving around a psychologic turning point in the life, in this case the fact of no longer being 20. Readers will be reminded of the decision of Harry Haller, the Steppenwolf of Herman Hesse, to commit suicide precisely on his 50th birthday.

S: What were your feelings then?

T: I was angry. I wanted to get out of there. I thought that first of all it was just a dream, that I was having a nightmare.

S: Were you angry that you had survived?

T: [Long pause.] I don't know. I don't think it was quite that. I think I was angry that I had to submit to this—to, you know, to all those procedures. And I was angry that I had complicated everything by this, by winding up in a hospital.

S: Then what happened?

T: Well, after that I was out of danger more or less at that point, and they pretty much let we wander around the hospital as I pleased. The next day there was some question about my husband letting me return home to the apartment, because he thought I was going to make another attempt and he couldn't bear to live with that. And it was just all up in the air; it was sort of like, well, you go and find a place to stay, and there was no place for me to stay. I don't know anyone here, and so it turned out that I was going to be staying in some sort of welfare kind of arrangement which was going to be fixed or arranged by the social worker.

S: So you felt at that point rejected by everyone.

T: Yeah . . . All of a sudden there I was out in the middle of nowhere without any money, and my husband wasn't going to let me come back to the house and I was desperate. And then I went into a terrible state.

S: Did he say that to you, that you couldn't return to the house?

T: Well, he said . . . he kept saying, "I'm not going to let you know, I'm going to keep you on tenterhooks. You should learn what it's like to

This penchant for complicating everything—messing up her life— is part of her inimical pattern. Her being married to that particular man is probably another manifestation of this inimicality.

The active withdrawal of support by a key "significant other" figure plunges her even deeper into a state of desperation-perturbation.

have to wait and to have patience."
S: In terms of what you had put
him through?
T: I guess. So that at this point I
was supposed to be making these
arrangements myself. I could
barely even speak, you know. The
social worker was calling various
agencies and then turning the
telephone over to me so I could tell
my story, and I could barely
remember my name—let alone my
date of birth or anything like that—
and I thought, my God in Heaven, I   *Here is heightened perturbation,*
can hardly even ... and I was not   *bordering on panic.*
functioning at all, and these people
are going to throw me into the
street. And I didn't want to go to a
psychiatric ward because I was
really frightened that I would wind
up ... that I would possibly have a
psychotic episode or something like
that.
S: Had that happened to you
before?
T: Almost, yes.
S: Had you had a neuropsychiatric
hospitalization?
T: Yes.
S: We'll talk more about that, but
not at this moment.
T: And I was so desperate I felt, my   *Very high perturbation:*
God, I can't face this thing—going   *desperation and "a whirlpool of*
out and being thrown out on the   *confusion." Two key items: (1) the*
street. And everything was like a   *intrusion of (dangerous)*
terrible sort of whirlpool of   *constricting, dichotomous thinking*
confusion. And I thought to myself,   *(". . . only one thing I can do . . . the*
there's only one thing I can do: I   *only way to lose consciousness . . .")*
just have to lose consciousness.   *and (2) the intrusion of the idea of*
That's the only way to get away   *cessation: to stop the flow of*
from it. The only way to lose   *unbearable anguish.*
consciousness. I thought, was to
jump off something good and high.
S: Did those thoughts actually go
through your mind?
T: I don't know. They didn't
actually go through my mind.
S: Then what happened?
T: I just figured I had to get outside,

but the windows were all locked. So
I managed to get outside.
S: How'd you do that?
T: I just slipped out. No one saw
me. And I got down to the ground
by walking across that catwalk
thing, sure that someone would see
me, you know, out of all those
windows. The whole building is
made of glass.
S: You were in a hospital gown
then?
T: Yes. And I just walked around
until I found this open staircase. As
soon as I saw it, I just made a
beeline right up to it. And then I got
to the fifth floor and everything just
got very dark all of a sudden, and
all I could see was this balcony.
Everything around it just blacked
out. It was just like a circle. That
was all I could see, was just the
balcony. And I went over it.
S: What did you do?
T: I climbed over it, and then I just
let go. [Sobs.] I was so desperate.
Just desperation. And the
horribleness and the quietness of it.
The quiet. Everything became so
quiet. There was no sound. And I
sort of went into slow motion as I
climbed over that balcony. I let go,
and it was like I was floating. I
blacked out. I don't remember any
part of the fall—just, just going. I
don't remember anything after
going over that balcony. I don't
remember crying or screaming. I
think I was panting from the
exertion and the strain of running
up all those stairs. And then, when I
woke up, I was having a dream,
which seemed very weird. At that
point I was in intensive care, and I
was looking at the patterns on the
ceiling . . .

Here is sharp ambivalence. There is
still the hope for intervention and
rescue (". . . sure that someone
would see me [and stop me]")
during the very time she is moving
across a narrow catwalk to her
death.

Here is a perfect, tragic but explicit,
gut-level description of what
psychic constriction really is.

The description of the falling is of
keen interest. Time is stopped.
There is no kaleidoscopic passing of
her life in review. She blacked out
and has no memory of her fall and
impact. Her injuries, while rather
serious—shattered left leg, ruptured
bladder, pneumothorax of one
lung—were miraculously light (not
one of her polished fingernails was
broken, nor was her beautiful face
scratched) considering her fall of
over 70 feet.

Orientations Toward Death: Subintentioned Death and Indirect Suicide

I t is both stimulating and depressing to contemplate the fact that at this period in man's history, when, at long last, one can find a few genuine indications of straightforward discussions and investigations of death, these pursuits come at the time of man's terrible new-found capacity to destroy his works and to decimate his kind. For these reasons, it may be said that a special kind of intellectual and affective permissiveness, born out of a sense of urgency, now exists for man's greater understanding of his own death and destruction.

For the past few years, a number of us engaged in activities related to the prevention of suicide have habitually looked upon instances of suicidal phenomena as manifestations of a major scourge, involving, as they inevitably do, untimely death for the victim and generally stigmatized lives for the survivors. My own special interest in the classification of death phenomena is one outcome of this group concern with suicidal behaviors. The purpose of this paper is to stimulate a rethinking of conventional notions of death and suicide. A further purpose is to attempt to create a psychologically oriented classification of death phenomena—an ordering based in large part on the role of the individual in his own demise.

Reflections on death, including suicide, are found in some of man's earliest written works. Death and suicide have been depicted and reified in various ways; numerous misconceptions have grown up around these topics. These proliferated intellectual overgrowths

---

From *The Study of Lives* (edited by Robert W. White), 1963, pp. 201-227. Reprinted with permission of Aldine-Atherton. This paper was written while the author was a U.S. Public Health Service Special Research Fellow (1961-1962), Harvard University, studying with Dr. Henry A. Murray.

are not the specimens that we wish to describe here. Rather, we have to see them as encumbering underbrush that must be cleared away before we can come to the heart of the problem. . . .

Cessation, Termination, Interruption, and Continuation

I n general, I have been critical of some current concepts relating to suicide and death. In this section I wish to propose a tentative psychological classification of all behaviors involving demise. Two sets of key concepts are involved: the first is made up of the terms cessation, termination, interruption, and continuation; the second, of the terms intentioned, subintentioned, unintentioned, and contraintentioned. At this point, our first tasks are those of definition.

Cessation

The key concept in this paper is the idea of "cessation."* In this context, cessation has a psychological, specifically introspective referent. Our definition of "cessation" is that it is the stopping of the potentiality of any (further) conscious experience. "Death"— some form of termination—is the universal and ubiquitous ending of all living things; but only man, by virtue of his verbally reportable introspective mental life, can conceptualize, fear, and suffer cessation. Cessation refers to the last line of the last scene of the last act of the last drama of that actor. It should be immediately obvious that different individuals—and any particular individual at different times—can have a variety of attitudes and orientations toward their cessations. The next section contains an explication of possible orientations toward cessation. Cessation is used here not as a synonym for the word death, but rather as its operationally defined substitute. It refers to the demise of the psychic processes— the final stopping of the individual consciousness, as far as we know.

---

*The term "cessation" is used in this present sense by Bridgman on at least two occasions, both in *The Intelligent Individual and Society* (New York: The Macmillan Company, 1938), pp. 169, 225.

Termination

The concept of "termination"—which is defined as the stopping of the physiological functions of the body—is needed because there can occur the stopping of the potentiality of conscious experience (cessation) which is not temporally coincident with the stopping of the functions of the body. Consider the report of the following incident: A young man was, while riding as a passenger on a motorcycle, hit by an automobile and thrown several yards through the air. He landed on his head at a curbside. At the hospital, this case was regarded as remarkable, because, although his skull was crushed and although he showed no evidence of any conscious experience and even had a rather complete absence of reflexes, he was kept alive for many days by means of intravenous feeding, catheter relief, and many other life-extending pieces of mechanical apparatus. Eventually he "expired." The conceptual point to be made in this context is that he suffered cessation the moment that his head hit the pavement. So, although he had ceased, he had not terminated, in that he continued to breathe. No one would have thought to suggest that he be buried or cremated as long as he was still breathing. A further point can be made: the operational definition (or criterion) for termination can be put at the stopping of the exchange of gases between the human organism and his environment, i.e., an individual may be said to be terminated when, if a mirror is put to his mouth, there is no frosting on the glass—the subsequent changes in the cells or other activities do not matter.* If cessation relates to the psychological personality, then termination has to do with the biological organism. It is useful to distinguish between cessation and termination. We all know that it is possible for an individual to put a gun to his head, planning to "blow his brains out" (termination) and yet *believe* that he will be at his own funeral, that he will be able to check whether or not his widow follows the instructions in his suicide note (without cessation). In order not to be entrapped by the confusion that exists in many minds concerning these two concepts, we must clarify them in our own.

---

* "I know when one is dead and when one lives; She's as dead as earth. Lend me a looking glass; if her breath will mist or stain the stone. Why, then she lives." *King Lear*, Act V, Scene 3.

Interruption

The third concept of this group is that of interruption, which relates not to termination but to cessation. If cessation has to do with the stopping of the potentiality of any conscious experience, then interruption is in a sense its opposite, in that "interruption" is defined as the stopping of consciousness with the actuality, and usually the expectation, of further conscious experiences. It is a kind of temporary cessation. The best example of an interruption state is being asleep; others are being under an anesthetic, in an alcoholic stupor, in a diabetic coma, in an epileptic seizure, and, on another level, being in a fugue, amnesic, or dissociative state. The primary purpose of introducing the notion of interruption states is to provide a concept whereby data—especially those which could be obtained from experimental situations—might serve as paradigms, analogues, models, or patterns for certain cessation conditions. For example—and more will be said about this later—it might be possible to devise paradigms having to do with sleep behavior that will give us fresh leads and new insights into suicidal behaviors, which a direct approach would not yield.

Continuation

When one works with suicidal people clinically and investigates, through "psychological autopsies," cases of suicide, one often gets the impression that individuals who, in point of fact, have killed themselves, have not necessarily "committed suicide." That is to say, in some cases, it seems that the person's intention was not to embrace death but rather to find surcease from external or internalized aspects of life. In the context of this paper, we shall call the process of living "continuation." Continuation can be defined as experiencing, in the absence of interruption, the stream of temporally contiguous conscious events. From this point of view, our lives are made up of a series of alternating continuation and interruption states.

One might find a group of nonlethally oriented "suicide attempters"—each of whom wished to postpone cessation—who, individually, might manifest quite different patterns of orientation toward continuation. The nuances of these patterns might well include the following:

1. patterns of ambivalence (coexistent wishes to live and to die,

including rescue fantasies, gambles with death, and cries for help);

2. the state of hopefulness or hopelessness, and accompanying feelings of psychological impotence;
3. patterns of self-righteousness, indignation, inner resourcefulness, defeat, and ennui;
4. orientations toward the next temporal interval, whether one of blandness, inertia, habit, interest, anticipation, expectation, or demand;
5. intensity of thought and action in relation to continuation, ranging from absent (no thought about it), through fleeting fantasy, concern, obsession, and rash behavior outburst, to deliberate performance.

Continuation is the coverse of cessation. It would be important to know, in any particular case, how an individual's attitudes toward continuation interacted with his orientations toward cessation. In addition to this, we could say that a comprehensive study of suicidal phenomena should include concern for nonsuicidal phenomena and such perverse questions as what a specific individual has to live for or why a specific individual does not commit suicide.

Basic Orientations Toward Cessation

The operation which gives meaning to the phrase "basic orientation toward cessation" has to do with the role of the individual in his own demise. By "role of the individual" is meant his overt and covert behaviors and nonbehaviors which reflect conscious and unconscious attributes relevant to his cessation. These include at least the following: his attitudes and beliefs about death, cessation, hereafter, and rebirth; his ways of thinking; his need systems, including his needs for achievement, affiliation, autonomy, and dominance; his dyadic relationships, especially the subtleties of dependencies and hostilities in relation to the significant people in his life; the hopefulness and hopelessness in the responses of these people to his cries for help; the constellation and balance of ego activity and ego passivity; his orientations toward continuation states. To know these facts about a person would well require a comprehensive psychological understanding of his personality.

Four subcategories relating to the role of the individual in his own demise are suggested: intentioned, subintentioned, unintentioned, and contraintentioned.

Intentioned

By intentioned, I refer to those cases in which the individual plays a direct and conscious role in his own demise. These cases do not refer to persons who wish for "death" or termination, but rather to those who actively precipitate their cessation. (Of course, cessation cannot be avoided by anyone. The entire issue is one of timing and involves postponing and hastening.) In terms of the traditional categories of death, no presently labeled accidental or natural deaths would be called intentioned, some homicidal deaths might be called intentioned, and most (but, importantly, not all) suicidal deaths would be called intentioned. In relation to the term "suicide," intentioned cases may be said to have *committed* suicide. We can list a number of subcategories: (1) Death-seekers; (2) Death-initiators; (3) Death-ignorers; and (4) Death-darers.

1. *Death seeker.* A Death-seeker is one who, during the time that he can be so labeled, has consciously verbalized to himself his wish for an ending to all conscious experience and behaves in order to achieve this end. The operational criteria for a Death-seeker lie not primarily in the method he uses—razor, barbiturate, carbon monoxide—but in the fact that the method *in his mind* is calculated to bring him cessation; and, whatever his rescue fantasies or cries for help may be, he does the act in such a manner and site that rescue (or intervention) is realistically unlikely or impossible. In all, he has a predominantly unambivalent intention or orientation toward cessation during that period. The phrase "during that period" is meant to convey the notion that individuals' orientations toward cessation shift and change over time.* A person who was a Death-seeker yesterday and made a most serious suicidal act then, could not today be forced to participate in activities that might cost him his life. It is known clinically that many individuals are "suicidal" for only a relatively brief period of time; so that if they can be given appropriate sanctuary, they will no longer seek death and will wish to continue to live as long as possible.

---

*The states described herein are meant to describe only the *current* status (vis-à-vis cessation) of the individual. Thus, one would, in any complete description of an individual, need also a biphasic taxonomy that describes the relatively chronic, pervasive, characterological, "presuicidal" aspects of his psychological make-up.

2. *Death-initiator*. A Death-initiator is a Death-seeker, but sufficiently different to warrant a separate label. A Death-initiator
believes that he will suffer cessation in the fairly near future—a
matter of days or weeks—or he believes that he is failing and, not
wishing to accommodate himself to a new (and less effective and
less virile) image of himself, does not wish to let "it" happen to him.
Rather *he* wants to play a role in its occurrence. Thus he will do it
for himself, at his own time, and on his own terms. In our investigations we find, an occasion, a case in which an older person,
hospitalized in a general medical hospital, in the terminal stages of
a fatal disease will, with remarkable and totally unexpected energy
and strength, take the tubes and needles out of himself, climb over
the bed rails, lift a heavy window, and throw himself to the ground
several stories below. What is most prototypical about such an
individual is that, when one looks at his previous occupational
history, one sees that he has never been fired—he has always quit.
In either case, the person ends up unemployed, but the role he has
played in the process is different.*

3. *Death-ignorer*. Consider the following suicide note: "Good-by
kid. You couldn't help it. Tell that brother of yours, when he gets to
where I'm going, I hope I'm a foreman down there; I might be able
to do something for him." Although it is true that suicide notes
which contain any reference to a hereafter, a continued existence,
or a reunion with dead loved ones are relatively very rare, it is also
true that some people who kill themselves believe, as part of their
total system of beliefs, that one can effect termination without
involving cessation. They seem to ignore the fact that, so far as we
know, termination always involves cessation. One can note that
even those in our contemporary society who espouse belief in a
hereafter as part of their religious tenets, still label a person who
has shot himself to death as suicidal. This is probably so primarily
because, whatever *really* happens after termination, the survivors
are still left to live (and usually to mourn) in the undeniable
physical absence of the person who killed himself. Thus, this

---

*Three very different examples of Death-initiators—all eminent men—are con-
tained in the following: Lael Tucker Wertenbaker, *Death of a Man* (New York:
Random House, 1957), pp. 174-181; Leicester Hemingway, *My Brother, Ernest
Hemingway* (New York: The World Publishing Company, 1962), p. 283; and Gerald
Holton, "Percy Williams Bridgman," reprinted in the *Bulletin of the Atomic Scien-
tists*, XVII, 2 (February, 1962), 22-23. It is interesting to contrast Hemingway's
attitude toward his failing body with that of Dr. Hans Zinsser: *As I Remember Him*
(Boston: Little, Brown and Company, 1940), pp. 200-201.

subcategory of Death-ignorer, or, perhaps better, Death-transcender, contains those persons who, from our point of view, effect their own termination and cessation but who, from their point of view, effect only their termination and continue to exist in some manner or another.

This paragraph is not meant to necessarily deny a (logical) possibility of continuation after cessation (life after death), but the concept of Death-ignoring (or something similar to it) is a firm necessity in any systematic classification of this type: otherwise we will put ourselves in the untenable position of making exactly comparable (1) a man's shotting his head off in the belief and hope that he will soon meet his dead wife in heaven and (2) a man's taking a trip from one city to another with the purpose and expectation of being reunited with his spouse. Obviously, these two acts are so vastly different in their effects (on the person concerned and on others who know him) that they cannot be equated. Therefore, independent of the individual's convictions that killing oneself does not result in cessation but is simply a transition to another life, we must superimpose our belief that cessation is necessarily final as far as the human personality which we can know is concerned.

4. *Death-darer.* A Death-darer is an individual who, to use gamblers' terms, bets his continuation (i.e., his life) on the objective probability of as few as five out of six chances that he will survive. Regardless of the outcome, an individual who plays Russian roulette is a Death-darer at that time. In addition to the objective probabilities that exist, the concept of a Death-darer also involves subjective probabilities of the same order of magnitude. Thus, a person with little skill as a pilot who attempts to fly an airplane, or one with unpracticed co-ordination who attempts to walk along the ledge of a roof of a tall building, may be classified as a Death-darer. The rule of thumb is that it is not what he does, but the background (of skill, prowess, and evaluation of his own abilities) against which he does it, that matters. In a sense the Death-darer is only a partial, or fractional, cessation-seeker; but since each lethal fraction contained within the gambling situation is completely lethal it seems most meaningful to classify such an act within the intention category.

Subintentioned

Subintentioned cessation behaviors relate to those instances in

which the individual plays an indirect, covert, partial, or unconscious role in his own demise. That individuals may play an
unconscious role in their own failures and act inimically to their
own best welfare seem to be facts too well documented from
psychoanalytic and general clinical practice to ignore. Often cessation is hastened by the individual's seeming carelessness, imprudence, foolhardiness, forgetfulness, amnesia, lack of judgment, or
other psychological mechanisms. This concept of subintentioned
demise is similar, in some ways, to Karl Menninger's concepts of
chronic, focal and organic suicides, except that Meninger's ideas
have to do with self-defeating ways of continuing to live, whereas
the notion of subintentioned cessation is a description of a way of
stopping the process of living. Included in this subintention category would be many patterns of mismanagement and brink-of-
death living which result in cessation. In terms of the traditional
classification of modes of death (natural, accident, suicide, and
homicide), some instances of all four types can be subsumed under
this category, depending on the particular details of each case. In
relation to the term suicide, subintentioned cases may be said to
have *permitted* suicide.

Subintentioned cessation involves what might be called the
psychosomatics of death: that is, cases in which essentially psychological processes (like fear, anxiety, derring-do, hate, etc.) seem to
play some role in exacerbating the catabolic or physiological
processes that bring on termination (and necessarily cessation), as
well as those cases in which the individual seems to play an
indirect, largely unconscious role in inviting or hastening cessation
itself.* The groups for the subintentioned category are, tentatively,
as follows: (1) Death-chancer; (2) Death-hastener; (3) Death-
capitulator; and (4) Death-experimenter.

1. *Death-chancer.* The Death-darer, Death-chancer, and Death-
experimenter are all on a continuum of chance expectation and
chance possibility of cessation. The difference lies in the combination of objective and subjective probabilities. If a Death-darer has
only five chances out of six of continuing, then a Death-chancer
would have chances significantly greater than that, but still involving a realistic risk of cessation. It should be pointed out that these

---

*See M.E. Wolfgang, "Suicide by Means of Victim-Precipitated Homicide," *Jour-
nal of Clinical and Experimental Psychopathology and Quarterly Review of Psychiatry and Neurology*, XX (1959), 335-349.

categories are largely independent of the method used, in that most methods (like the use of razor blades or barbiturates) can, depending on the exact place of the cut, the depth of the cut, and the realistic and calculated expectations for intervention and rescue by others, legitimately be thought of as intentioned, subintentioned, unintentioned, or contraintentioned—depending on these circumstances. Individuals who "leave it up to chance," who "gamble with death,"* who "half-intend to do it" are the subintentioned Death-chancers.

2. *Death-hastener*. The basic assumption is that in all cessation activities the critical question (on the assumption that cessation will occur to everyone) is when, so that, in a sense, all intentioned and subintentioned activities are hastening. The Death-hastener refers to the individual who unconsciously exacerbates a physiological disequilibrium so that his cessation (which would, in ordinary terms, be called a natural death) is expedited. This can be done either in terms of the "style" in which he lives (the abuse of his body, usually through alcohol, drugs, exposure, or malnutrition) or, in cases where there is a specific physiological imbalance, through the mismanagement of prescribed remedial procedures. Examples of the latter would be the individual with cirrhosis who "mismanages" his alcoholic intake, the Berger's disease patient who "mismanages" his nicotine intake. Very closely allied to the Death-hastener is the Death-facilitator, who, while he is ill and his psychic energies are low, is somehow more-than-passively unresisting to cessation, and "makes it easy" for termination (and accompanying cessation) to occur. Some unexpected deaths in hospitals may be of this nature. The excellent recent paper of Weisman and Hackett explores this area.**

3. *Death-capitulator*. A Death-capitulator is a person who, by virtue of some strong emotion, usually his fear of death, plays a psychological role in effecting his termination. In a sense, he gives in to death or he scares himself to death. This type of death includes voodoo deaths; the type of death reported among Indians and Mexicans from southwestern United States railroad hospitals, where the patients thought that people who went to hospitals went

---

See J.M.A. Weiss, "The Gamble with Death in Attempted Suicide," *Psychiatry*, XX (1957), 17-25.

**Avery D. Weisman and Thomas P. Hackett in "Predilection to Death: Death and Dying as a Psychiatric Problem," *Psychosomatic Medicine*, XXIII, 3 (May 1961), 232-256.

there to die, and being hospitalized was thus cause in itself for great alarm; and some of the cases reported from Boston by Weisman and Hackett. All these individuals play a psychological role in the psychosomatics of their termination and cessation.

4. *Death-experimenter.* A Death-experimenter is a person who often lives "on the brink of death," who consciously wishes neither interruption nor cessation, but—usually by use of (or addiction to) alcohol and/or barbiturates—seems to wish a chronically altered, usually befogged continuation state. Psyde-experimenters seem to wish to remain conscious but to be benumbed or drugged. They will often "experiment" with their self-prescribed dosages (always in the direction of increasing the effect of the dosage), taking some chances of extending the benumbed conscious states into interruption (coma) states and even taking some chances (usually without much concern, in a kind of lackadaisical way) of running some minimal but real risk of extending the interruption states into cessation.

Unintentioned

Unintentioned cessation describes those occurrences in which, for all intents and purposes, the person psychologically plays no significant role in his own demise. He is, at the time of his cessation, "going about his business" (even though he may be lying in a hospital), with no conscious intention of effecting or hastening cessation and no strong conscious drive in this direction. What happens is that "something from the outside"—the outside of his mind—occurs. This "something" might be a cerebral-vascular accident, a myocardial infarction, a neoplastic growth, some malfunction, some catabolism, some invasion—whether by bullet or by virus—which, for him, has lethal consequences. "It" happens to "him." Inasmuch as all that anyone can do in regard to cessation is to attempt some manipulation along a temporal dimension (i.e., to hasten or to postpone it), one might suppose that unintentioned is synonymous only with "postponer," but it appears that there are other possible attitudes—welcoming, accepting, resisting, disdaining, etc.—all within the unintentioned category.

In terms of the traditional categories of death, most natural, accidental, and homicidal deaths would be called unintentioned, and no presently labeled suicidal deaths would be so called. In relation to the term "suicidal," unintentioned cases may be said to have *omitted* suicide.

The categories for unintentioned cessation are (1) Death-welcomer; (2) Death-acceptor; (3) Death-postponer; (4) Death-disdainer; and (5) Death-fearer.

1. *Death-welcomer.* A Death-welcomer is one who, although playing no discernible (conscious or unconscious) role in either hastening or facilitating his own cessation, could honestly report an introspective position of welcoming the end to his life. Very old people, especially after a long, painful, debilitating illness, report that they would welcome "the end."

2. *Death-acceptor.* The slight difference between a Death-welcomer and a Death-acceptor lies in the nuance of activity and passivity that distinguishes them. The Death-acceptor is one who has accepted the imminence of his cessation and "is resigned to his own fate." In this, he may be relatively passive, philosophical, resigned, heroic, realistic, or mature, depending on "the spirit" in which this enormous acceptance is made.

3. *Death-postponer.* Most of the time most of us are acute Death-postponers. Death-postponing is the habitual, indeed the unthinking, orientation of most humans toward cessation. The Death-postponer is one who, to the extent that he is oriented toward or concerned with cessation at all, wishes that it would not occur in anything like the foreseeable future and further wishes that it would not occur for as long as possible. (This Death-postponing orientation should not be confused with the ubiquitous human fantasies of immortality.)

4. *Death-disdainer.* Some individuals, during those moments when they consciously contemplate cessation, are disdainful of the concept and feel that they are above being involved in the cessation of the vital processes that it implies. They are, in a sense, supercilious toward death. It may well be that most young people in our culture, independent of their fears about death, are habitually Death-disdainers, as well they might be—for a while.*

5. *Death-fearer.* A Death-fearer is one who is fearful of death and of the topics relating to death. He may literally be phobic about this topic.** He fights the notion of cessation, seeing reified death as a

---

*See P. Schilder and D. Wechsler, "The Attitudes of Children toward Death," *Journal of Genetic Psychology.* XLV (1934), 405-451, and Maria Nagy, "The Child's View of Death," in H. Feifel, ed., *The Meaning of Death*, pp. 79-98.

**For example, W.A. Swanberg in *Citizen Hearst* (New York: Charles Scribner's Sons, 1961, p. 455) says: "Hearst . . . had a violent aversion for mortality, and there was an unwritten law never to mention death in his presence."

feared and hated enemy. This position may be related to conscious
wishes for omnipotence and to great cathexis to one's social and
physical potency. Hypochondriacs, fearing illnesses and assault,
are perhaps also Death-fearers. (A person who, when physically
well, is a Death-fearer might, when physically ill, become a Death-
facilitator.)

Imagine five people, all older men on the same ward of a hospital,
all dying of cancer, none playing an active or unconscious role in
his own cessation. Yet it is still possible to distinguish among them
different orientations toward cessation: One wishes not to die and
is exerting his "will to live" (Death-postponer); another is resigned
to his cessation Death-acceptor); the third is disdainful of what is
occurring to him and will not believe that death can "take him"
(Death-disdainer); still another, although not taking any steps in
the direction of hastening his end, does at this point in his illness
welcome it (Death-welcomer); and the fifth is most fearful about the
topic of death and the implication of cessation and forbids anyone
to speak of it in his presence (Death-fearer).

Contraintentioned

It is, of course, possible to shout "Fire!" in the absence of a
conflagration, or "Stop thief!" in the absence of a crime. It is also
possible, figuratively or literally, to shout or to murmur—the
intensity of the cry does not seem to matter in some cases—
"Suicide!" in the clear absence of any lethal intention. (I shall, of
course, eschew the words "suicide attempt" and "suicide threat,"
having already indicated that either of these can range from great
lethal intent, through ambivalent lethal intent, to no lethal intent.)
One common result of shouting "Fire! or "Stop thief" is that these
calls mobilize others; indeed, they put society (or certain members
of society) in a position where it has no choice but to act in certain
directions. An individual who uses the semantic blanket of "Suicide!" with a conscious absence of any lethal intention I shall
term as one who has employed contraintentioned—advertently
noncessation—behavior. From a strictly logical point of view, it
might be argued that contraintentioned behaviors belong within
the unintentioned category. I believe, however, that there are
sufficient reasons to warrant a separate category, if only to point up
the fact that individuals can usurp the labels and the semantic
trappings of death, especially of suicide and, at the same time, have

a clear, conscious intention not to commit suicide and not to run any risk of cessation.

Among the contraintentioned individuals there are, by definition, no cessation or related postmortem states and hence no comparable tradition modes of death. In relation to the term suicide, contraintention cases may be said to have *remitted* (in the sense of having "refrained from") suicide.

The subcategories that we distinguish among the contraintentioned cases are (1) Death-feigner and (2) Death-threatener.

1. *Death-feigner.* A Death-feigner is one who feigns or simulates what appears to be a self-directed advertent movement toward cessation. Examples are the ingesting of water from a previously emptied iodine bottle or using a razor blade with no lethal or near-lethal possibility or intent. Death-feigning involves some overt behavior on the part of the individual.

2. *Death-threatener.* A Death-threatener is a person who with the conscious intention of avoiding cessation, uses the threat of his cessation (and the other's respect for that threat) with the aim of achieving some of the secondary gains which go with cessation-oriented behavior. These gains usually have to do with activating other persons—usually the "significant other" person in the neurotic dyadic relationship in which the individual is involved.

Two additional comments, both obvious, should be made about contraintentioned behavior. The first is that what are ordinarily called "suicide attempts" may range in their potential lethality from absent to severe. I do not wish to imply for a moment that all so-called suicide attempts should be thought of as contraintentioned: quite the contrary. Thus, each case of barbiturate ingestion or wrist cutting, or even of the use of carbon monoxide in an auto, must be evaluated in terms of the details of that case, so that it can be assessed accurately—as of that time—in terms of its intentioned, subintentioned, unintentioned and contraintentioned components. The second comment is that those who work with people who have "attempted suicide," especially those people seen as having manifested contraintentioned behavior, must guard against their own tendencies to assume a prejorative attitude toward these behaviors. It is all too easy to say that an individual *only* attempted suicide or to dismiss the case as beneath the need for human compassion, if one assesses the act as contraintentioned. It should be obvious that *no* act which involves, even merely semantically, cessation behavior is other than a genuine psychiatric crisis. Too often we confuse treatment and suicidal individuals with attending to the physical trauma, forgetting that meaningful treatment has to be essentially in terms of the person's personality and the frustrations, duress, fears, and threats which he experiences in his living relationships. An unquestioned contraintentioned act merits fully as much professional attention as any other maladaptive behavior; a cry for help should never be disregarded, not only for humanitarian reasons, but also because we know that the unattended cries tend to become more shrill, and the movement on the lethality scale from cry to cry is, unfortunately, in the lethal direction. . . .

An Example of a Subintentioned Death; an Indirect Suicide

It might be most appropriate to conclude this paper by presenting, by way of example, some excerpts from a singularly interesting case. The study I have chosen is taken from a uniquely comprehensive study of death and lives by Herman Melville. It is the case of the equivocal death— was it accident, suicide, or what?—of Melville's tortured, obsessively possessed, fury-driven, cetusized man: Captain Ahab of the *Pequod*.*

The procedure called the "psychological autopsy" (used at the Suicide Prevention Center) involves obtaining psychological data about the behaviors and statements of the deceased in the days before his death, from which information an extrapolation of intention is made over the moments of, and the moments directly preceding, his cessation. In the case of Captain Ahab, I shall proceed as though I were preparing a report for an imaginary Nantucket coroner, including some sort of recommendation as to what labelings would be the most appropriate on his imaginary death certificate. The focus will be an attempt to come to some kind of resolution concerning Ahab's intention types and Death cate-

---

*The reader is referred to Henry A. Murray's masterful psychological studies of Melville: "In Nomine Diaboli," in *Moby-Dick Centennial Essays* (Dallas, Texas: Southern Methodist University Press, 1953), pp. 3-29, originally published in *New England Quarterly*, XXIV (1951), 435-452; Milton R. Stern (ed.), *Discussions of Moby Dick* (Boston, Massachusetts: D.C. Heath and Company, 1960), pp. 25-34; and Richard Chase (ed.), *Melville: A Collection of Critical Essays* (Englewood Cliffs, New Jersey: Prentice-Hall, Inc. 1962), pp. 62-74; and his "Introduction" to Melville's *Pierre, or The Ambiguities* (New York: Hendricks House, 1949), pp. xiii-ciii. All these pieces are reproduced in E.S. Shneidman (Ed.) *Endeavors in Psychology: Selections from the Personology of Henry A. Murray*. New York: Harper & Row, 1981.

gories. But first, some facts: specifically how did the end of his life occur?

Facts

For Ahab's death, we have the following account (from Chapter 135) of his last actions: "The harpoon was darted; the stricken whale flew forward; with igniting velocity the line ran through the groove;—ran foul. Ahab stooped to clear it; he did clear it; but the flying turn caught him round the neck, and noiselessly as Turkish mutes bowstring their victim, he was shot out of the boat, ere the crew knew he was gone. . . ." On first thought, it might sound as though Ahab's death were pure accident, an unintentioned death, the cessation of a Death-postponer; but let us see where our second thoughts lead us. Perhaps there is more.

Background

It is possible to view *Moby Dick* as a great, sonorous Mahlerlike symphony—*Das Lied von der See*—not primarily about the joy of life nor the pessimism engendered by a crushing fate, but rather as a dramatic and poetic explication of the psychodynamics of death. And, within the context of this thought, is it not possible that Moby Dick, the great *white* whale, represents the punishment of death itself? In Chapter 28, when Ahab makes his first appearance on the *Pequod* at sea, the word "white" is used three times in one paragraph to describe Ahab: a head-to-toe scar on Ahab's body, "lividly whitish"; an allusion to a "white sailor," in the context of Captain Ahab's being laid out for burial; and "the barbaric white leg upon which he partly stood." Everywhere, reference to the pallor of death; and if there is still any question, the case for "white death" is made explicit in the discussion of the whiteness of the whale (Chapter 12), in which we are told: "It cannot well be doubted, that the one visible quality in the aspect of the dead which most appalls the gazer, is the marble pallor lingering there; as if indeed that pallor were as much like the badge of consternation in the other world, as of mortal trepidation here. And from that pallor of the dead, we borrow the expressive hue of the shroud in which we wrap them. Nor even in our superstitions do we fail to throw the same snowy mantel round our phantoms; all ghosts rising in a milk-white fog—Yea, while these terrors seize us, let us add that even the king of terrors, when personified by the evangelist rides on his pallid horse."

And if the great white whale is death then is not the sea itself the vessel of death? Melville sets this tone for his entire heroic narrative in his stunning opening passage:

> Call me Ishmael. Some years ago—never mind how long precisely—having little or no money in my purse, and nothing particular to interest me on shore, I thought I would sail about a little and see the watery part of the world. It is a way of driving off the spleen, and regulating the circulation. Whenever I find myself growing grim about the mouth; whenever it is a damp, drizzly, November in my soul; whenever I find myself involuntarily pausing before coffin warehouses, and bringing up the rear of every funeral I meet; and especially whenever my hypos get such an upper hand of me, that it requires a strong moral principle to prevent me from deliberately stepping into the street, and methodically knocking people's hats off—then, I account it high time to get to sea as soon as I can. This is my substitute for pistol and ball. With a philosophical flourish Cato throws himself upon his sword; I quietly take to the ship.

And again, much later, in the description of the blacksmith (Chapter 112), we read:

> Death seems the only desirable sequel for a career like this; but Death is only a launching into the region of the strange Untried; it is but the first salutation to the possibilities of the immense Remote, the Wild, the Watery, the Unshored: therefore, to the death-longing eyes of such men, who still have left in them some interior compunctions against suicide, does the all-contributed and all-receptive ocean alluringly spread forth his whole plain of unimaginable, taking terrors and wonderful, new-life adventures; and from the hearts of infinite Pacifics, the thousand mermaids sing to them—"Come hither, broken-hearted; here is another life without the guilt of intermediate death; here are wonders supernatural, without dying for them. Come hither! bury thyself in a life which, to your now equally abhorred and abhorring, landed world, is more oblivious than death. Come hither! put up *thy* grave-stone, too, within the churchyard, and come hither, till we marry thee!"

If any case is to be made for subintention—Death-chancing, Death-hastening, Death-capitulating, Death-experimenting behavior patterns—then, at the least, two further background issues need to be involved: the concept of unconscious motivation and the concept of ambivalence. Ahab's chronicler would not have, in principle, resisted the concept of subintention, on the grounds of its involving unconscious motivation, for (in Chapter 41) he says:

> Such a crew, so officered, seemed specially picked and packed
> by some infernal fatality to help him to his monomaniac
> revenge. How it was that they so aboundingly responded to the
> old man's ire—by what evil magic their souls were possessed,
> that at times his hate seemed almost theirs; the White Whale as
> much their insufferable foe as his; how all this came to be—
> what the White Whale was to them, or how to their unconscious
> understandings, also, in some dim, unsuspected way, he might
> have seemed the gliding great demon of the seas of life—all this
> to explain, would be to dive deeper than Ishmael can go. The
> subterranean miner that works in us all, how can one tell
> whither leads his shaft by the ever shifting, muffled sound of
> his pick?

That which is most sharply and most accurately characteristic of
the subintentioned person—namely, the ubiquitous ambivalence,
the pervasive psychological coexistence of logical incompatibles—
is seen vividly in the following internal dialogue of life and death,
of flesh and fixture (as reported in Chapter 51) within Ahab:

> Walking the deck with quick, side-lunging strides, Ahab
> commanded the t'gallant sails and royals to be set, and every
> stunsail spread. The best man in the ship must take the helm.
> Then, with every mast-head manned, the piled-up craft rolled
> down before the wind. The strange, upheaving, lifting tendency
> to the taff-rail breeze filling the hollows of so many sails, made
> the buoyant, hovering deck to feel like air beneath the feet;
> while still she rushed along, as if two antagonistic influences
> were struggling in her—one to mount directly to heaven, the
> other to drive yawningly to some horizontal goal. And had you
> watched Ahab's face that night, you would have thought that in
> him also two different things were warring. While his one live
> leg made lively echoes along the deck, every stroke of his dead
> limb sounded like a coffin-tap. On life and death this old man
> walked.

And within Ahab, toward Moby Dick, there were deep ambiguities.

Method

In any psychological autopsy it is important to examine the
method or the instrument of death and, especially, the victim's
understandings and subjective estimations of its lethal works.

Ahab was garroted by a free-swinging whale line. We are warned (in Chapter 60) that "... the least tangle or kink in the coiling would, in running out, infallibly take somebody's arm, leg, or entire body off ..."; we are forewarned "... of this man or that man being taken out of the boat by the line, and lost"; and we are warned again, "All men live enveloped in whale lines. All are born with halters round their necks; but it is only when caught in the swift, sudden turn of death, that mortals realize the silent, subtle, ever-present perils of life." Ahab knew all this; nor was he a careless, accident-prone man. The apothecary knows his deadly drugs; the sportsman knows the danger of his weapons; the whaler captain— that very whaler captain who, instead of remaining on his quarter-deck, jumped to "the active perils of the chase" in a whaleboat manned by his "smuggled on board" crew—ought to know his whale lines.

Questions

Having described the precise circumstances of Ahab's death, and having mentioned some background issues deemed to be relevant, I would now pose some questions concerning his demise: Was Ahab's death more than simple accident? Was there more intention than unintention? Was Ahab's orientation in relation to death entirely that of Death-postponing? Are there discernible subsurface psychological currents that can be fathomed and charted, and is there related information that can be dredged and brought to the surface? Specifically, can Ahab's death be described as victim-precipitated homicide; that is, is this an instance in which the victim stands up to subjectively calculated overwhelming odds, inviting destruction by the other? Let us see.

Extracts

Ahab led a fairly well-documented existence, especially insofar as the dark side of his life was concerned. *Moby Dick* abounds with references to various funereal topics: sleep, coffins, burials, soul, life-after-death, suicide, cemeteries, death, and rebirth.

But—as in a psychological autopsy—we are primarily interested in interview data from everyone who had known the deceased, especially in what our informants can tell us about Ahab's personality, insofar as his orientations toward death are known. It should be recognized that in some important ways Captain Ahab's psychological autopsy will be a truncated and atypical one, especially with respect to the range of informants; there is no information from spouse, parents, progeny, siblings, collaterals, neighbors; there are only mates, some of the more articulate shipboard subordinates, captains of ships met at sea, and, with terrifying biblical certitude, Elijah.

As we know, all the possible informants, listed below, save Ishmael, perished with Captain Ahab and are technically not available to interview. Only Ishmael's observations are direct; all else is secondhand through Ishmael, colored by Ishmael, and perhaps with no more veridicality than Plato's reports of Socrates. We shall have to trust Ishmael to be an accurate and perceptive reporter.

Our primary informant, Ishmael, reflected about Captain Ahab in twenty-five separate chapters (specifically chapters 16, 22, 27, 28, 30, 33, 34, 36, 41, 44, 46, 50, 51, 52, 73, 100, 106, 115, 116, 123, 126, 128, 130, 132, and 133). Starbuck, the chief mate of the *Pequod*, is next: there are nine separate encounters with, or reports about, his captain (in chapters 36, 38, 51, 118, 119, 123, 132, 134, and 135). Next is Stubb, the second mate, with seven separate anecdotes (to be found in chapters 28, 31, 36, 73, 121, 134, and 135). All the others are represented by one or two bits of information apiece: Elijah (in chpaters 19 and 21); Gabriel of the *Jeroboam* (Chapter 71); Bunger, the ship's surgeon of the *Samuel Enderby* (100); the blacksmith (113); the Captain of the *Bachelor* (115); Flask, the third mate (121); the Manxman (125); and the carpenter (127).

Knowing that the limitations of space simply do not permit me to document the essence of each informant's remarks, either with appropriate quotations or abbreviated résumés, how can I summarize all the data? Perhaps my best course would be to concentrate on the general features that one would look for in any psychological autopsy. Thus, the information distilled from interviews with Ishmael, Starbuck, Stubb, and all the others, might, in a dialogue of questions and answers, take the following form.

1. Hidden psychosis? Not at the beginning of the voyage, but certainly at the end (and indeed from Chapter 36 on—"the chick that's in him picks the shell. 'Twill soon be out."), the madness in Ahab was blatant, open, known. His monomania was the official creed of his ship. Along with his other symptoms, his psychiatric syndrome was crowned with a paranoid fixation. But what matters

in Ahab is not so much the bizarrely shaped psychological iceberg which many saw above the surface, but rather the hugeness of the gyroscopically immovable subsurface mass of other-destruction and self-destruction. We know the poems about fire and ice. Ahab is a torrid, burning, fiery iceberg.

2. Disguised depression? Ahab was openly morbid and downcast. His was not exactly psychotic depression, nor can we call it reactive depression, for it transcended the bounds of that definition. Perhaps best it might be called a "character depression," in that it infused his brain like the let-go blood from a series of small strokes in the hemisphere.

3. Talk of death? The morbid talk of death and killing runs through reports about Ahab like an *idée fixe*.

4. Previous suicide attempts? None is reported.

5. Disposition of belongings? Ahab, after forty solitary years at sea, had little in the way of self-possessions or interpersonal belongings. His wife, he said, was already a widow; his interest in the possible profits from the voyage was nil: his withdrawal from meaningful material possessions (and his loss of joy with them) is perhaps best indicated by his flinging his "still lighted pipe into the sea" and dashing his quadrant to the deck—both rash acts for a sailor-captain.

In Ahab's conscious mind, he wanted to kill—but have we not said that self-destruction can be other-destruction in the 180th degree? Figuratively speaking, the barb of the harpoon was pointed toward him; his brain thought a thrust, but his arm executed a retroflex. Was his death "accident"? If he had survived his psychodynamically freighted voyage and had returned unharmed to Nantucket's pier, *that* would have been true accident. Men can die for nothing—most men do: but some few big-jointed men can give their lives for an internalized something: Ahab would not have missed this opportunity for the world.

What further evidence can be cited bearing on the issue of subintentioned cessation? With his three harpooners before him, with their harpoons turned up like goblets, Arab (in Chapter 36) commands them, in this maritime immolation scene, as follows: "Drink, ye harpooneers! drink and swear, ye men that man the deathful whaleboat's bow—Death to Moby Dick! God hunt us all, if we do not hunt Moby Dick to his death!" Kill or be killed: punish or be retributed: murder or suicide—how the two are interwined.

In Ahab's case, we have no suicide note or other holograph of death, but, *mirabile dictu,* we do have (in Chapter 135) Ahab's last thoughts:

> I turn my body from the sun.... Oh, lonely death on lonely life! Oh, now I feel my topmost grief. Ho, ho! from all your furtherest bounds, pour ye now in, ye bold billows of my whole foregone life, and top this one piled comber of my death! Towards thee I roll, thou all-destroying but unconquering whale; to the last I grapple with thee; from hell's heart I stab at thee: for hate's sake I spit my last breath at thee Sink all coffins and all hearses to one common poll! and since neither can be mine, let me now tow to pieces, while still chasing thee, though tied to thee, thou damned whale! *Thus,* I give up my spear!

What is to be particularly noted in this is the prescience of Ahab. "I spit my last breath at thee," he says. How does he know that it is to be his *last* breath? Where are the sources of his premonitions? What are the contents of his subintentions? Does this not remind us of Radney, the chief mate of the *Town-Ho* (Chapter 54) who behaved as if he "sought to run more than half way to meet his doom"? Is this not exactly what the tantalizer says to his "all-destroying but unconquering" executioner in cases of victim-precipitated homicide?

Recommendation

It is suggested that Captain Ahab's demise was goal-seeking behavior that made obsessed life *or* subintentioned death relatively unimportant to him, compared with the great press for the discharge of his monomania of hate. He dared, and made, that murderous death-white whale kill him. He could not rest until he was so taken. (Did Satan *provoke* God into banishing him?) Ahab invited cessation by the risks that he ran: he was a Death-chancer. He permitted suicide. Consider Ahab's psychological position: what could he have done, to what purpose would any further voyages have been, if he *had* killed the symbol of his search? It was, from Ahab's point of view, the time; and in his unconscious wish, it was the "appropriate death."

Suicide among the Gifted

T he two principal assertions in this paper are (a) that discernible early prodromal clues to adult suicide may be found in longitudinal case history data and (b) that it is useful to conceptualize these premonitory clues in terms of *perturbation* and *lethality*.

The data from which evidence for these assertions was obtained are those of the longitudinal study of 1,528 gifted people initiated by Lewis M. Terman in 1921. Terman and his co-workers searched the public schools of the cities of California for exceptionally bright youngsters. His purposes were "to discover what gifted children are like as children, what sort of adult they become, and what some of the factors are that influence their development" (Oden, 1968). That study, begun over a half-century ago, continues to this day.

Of the original 1,528 subjects, 857 were males and 671 were females. The sample was composed of children (mean age 9.7 years) with Stanford-Binet I.Q.'s of 140 or higher—the mean I.Q. was over 150—and an older group of high school students (mean age 15.2 years) who scored within the top 1 percent on the Terman Group Test of Mental Ability. The present analysis will be limited to male subjects, of whom approximately 80 percent were born between 1905 and 1914.

An enormous amount of data has been collected. At the time of the original investigation in 1921-22, the information included a developmental record, health history, medical examination, home and family background, school history, character trait ratings and personality evaluations by parents and teachers, interest tests, school achievement tests, and the like. Subsequently, there has

From *Life-Threatening Behavior*, Spring, 1971, Vol. 1, No. 1, pp. 23-45. Reprinted with permission. This study was conducted while the author was a Fellow at the Center for Advanced Study in the Behavioral Sciences, 1969-70. Arrangements were made for confidential access to the research records by Professor Robert R. Sears who, with Professor Lee J. Cronbach, is one of the two scientific executors of the Terman Study. The data themselves are the property of Stanford University. The author is especially grateful to Mrs. Melita Oden and Mrs. Sheila Buckholtz, long-time staff members of the Gifted Study, for their extensive help in preparing relevant data for his use and for advice and guidance along the way.

been a long series of systematic follow-ups by mail or by personal field visits: in 1924, 1925, 1936, 1940, 1945, 1950, 1955, and 1960. Another follow-up study is planned for the near future. In the field studies (1921, 1927, 1940, and 1950), subjects and their families were interviewed, and data from intelligence tests, personality tests, and questionnaires were obtained.

The Terman studies have catalyzed two generations of thought, research, attitudinal changes, and educational developments. Detailed descriptions of the subjects at various ages, as well as summaries of the important findings, are available in a series of publications authored by Professor Terman and his chief co-worker, Melita Oden (Oden, 1968; Terman, 1925, 1940; Terman & Oden, 1947, 1959). Among longitudinal studies (Stone & Onque, 1959) the Terman Study is unique in many ways, including the extent to which its staff has continued to maintain contact with the subjects for over a half a century. As of 1960, only 1.7 percent of the 1,528 subjects had been lost entirely.

Almost everyone in the psychological and pedagogical worlds now knows the basic findings of the Terman Study: that intellectually gifted children—far from being, as was once thought, spindly, weak, and maladjusted or one-sided—are, on the whole, more physically and mentally healthy and successful than their less-than-gifted counterparts. An unusual mind, a vigorous body, and a well-adjusted personality are not incompatible.*

A mortality summary for the Terman gifted group is as follows: In 1960—when the median age was 49.6—there had been 130 known deaths, 83 male and 47 female. The mortality rate was 9.8 percent for males and 7.2 percent for females—8.6 percent for the total group. According to Dublin's life tables (Dublin, Lotka, & Spiegelman, 1949), 13.9 percent of white males, 10.1 percent of white females, and 12 percent of a total cohort who survive to age 11 will have died before age 50. In 1960, the figures indicated a favorable mortality rate in the Terman group lower than the general white population of the same age.

---

*As part of the Terman Study of the Gifted, Catharine M. Cox (1926) completed a comprehensive retrospective study of the childhood intelligence of 301 historically eminent men born after 1450. Of the individuals discussed in her study, 119 were thought to have I.Q.'s of 140 or higher. (As examples, here are some names—1 person in each of the five-step I.Q. intervals from 140 to 190: Carlyle, Jefferson, Descartes, Hume, Pope, J. Q. Adams, Voltaire, Schelling, Pascal, Leibnitz, and J. S. Mill.) As to suicide among this extraordinary group, so far as can be ascertained, only 1 of the 301 eminent men died by killing himself—Thomas Chatterton, at age 17.

By 1960, 110 of the 130 Terman group deaths—61 percent—had been due to natural causes. (Cardiovascular diseases ranked first with males, and cancer was first among females.) Accidents accounted for 19 male deaths, while only 5 females died in accidents. Five men had lost their lives in World War II. There were no homicide victims. One death was equivocal as to mode and could not be classified. As of 1960, suicide was responsible for 14 male and 8 females deaths; by 1970 there were 28 known deaths by suicide—20 men and 8 women.

An inspection of the listing of suicidal deaths (Table 1) suggested that there were several subgroups: student suicides, 30- and 40-year suicides, and middle-age suicides. Among the 28 suicides—of both sexes, ranging in age from 18 to 63 (a 45-year span), year of death from 1928 to 1968 (40 years), using a variety of lethal methods (pills, poison, drowning, guns)—there was a subgroup of 5 persons—numbers 14 to 18—all of whom were male, Caucasian, with I.Q.'s over 140, born about the same time (between 1907 and 1916), four of whom committed suicide within a year of each other (1965 or 1966), were in the "middle period" of their lives (ages at death 43, 50, 51, 53, and 58), and used the same method (all gunshot). This special subgroup seemed to offer a unique opportunity for an especially intensive investigation.*

A listing of all those subjects who had died indicated that there were 10 other males, born about the same time (1910 to 1914) as the 5 suicides, who had died of natural causes (either cancer or heart disease) during the same years that four of the five suicides had killed themselves (1965-66). The opportunity for a natural experiment, using blind analyses, was evident.

Thirty cases were selected to include the five suicides, the 10 natural deaths, and 15 individuals who were still alive. The latter two subgroups were matched with the five suicides in terms of age, occupational level, and father's occupational level. That these three subgroups are fairly well matched is indicated by the information

---

*In the technical literature on suicide, one does not find many anamnestic or case history reports for individuals who have *committed* suicide. (Materials for attempted suicides are another story; the data for them are far more plentiful.) Only four sources—spread over a half-century—come to mind: Ruth Cavan's (1928, pp. 198-248) extensive diaries of two young adults, Binswanger's (1958) detailed report of 33-year-old Ellen West, Kobler and Stotland's (1964, pp. 98-251) extensive reports of four hospitalized patients—ages 23, 34, 37, and 56—in a "dying hospital," all of whom committed suicide within the same month, and Alvarez' (1961) annotated bibliography.

Table 1

The 28 Suicides in the Terman Study as of 1970

	Age at Suicide	Year of Birth	Year of Suicide	Marital Status	Education	Occupational Level*	Method of Suicide
Men							
1.	18	1910	1928	S	High School	S	Poison
2.	19	1916	1935	S	2 yrs. college	V	Gunshot
3.	24	1908	1932	S	AB+	Grad S	Drowning
4.	28	1910	1938	S	MA	II	Poison
5.	33	1913	1946	M,D,M	High School	III	Barbiturate
6.	34	1913	1947	S	2 yrs. college	III	Carbon monoxide
7.	35	1904	1939	S	Ph.D.	I	Gunshot
8.	37	1909	1946	M	1½ yrs. coll.	II	Poison
9.	42	1905	1947	M	2 yrs. college	II	Not known
10.	42	1916	1958	M,D,M,D	AB + 3 yrs.	I	Barbiturate
11.	45	1911	1956	M	3 yrs. college	II	Barbiturate
12.	45	1911	1956	M	AB,MA,LLB	IV	Carbon monoxide
13.	45	1913	1958	M	MD+	I	Poison
14.	43	1910	1953	M[4],D[4]	2 yrs. college	II	Gunshot
15.	50	1916	1965	M,D	BS	Inc.	Gunshot
16.	51	1915	1966	M,D,M	High School	III	Gunshot
17.	53	1913	1966	M	LLB	I	Gunshot
18.	58	1907	1966	M[3],D[3]	2 yrs. college	I	Gunshot
19.	61	1905	1966	S	MA	Rest (I)	Barbiturate
20.	63	1905	1968	M,D,M	Ph.D.	I	Barbiturate

Table 1 (Continued)

The 28 Suicides in the Terman Study as of 1970

	Age at Suicide	Year of Birth	Year of Suicide	Marital Status	Education	Occupational Level*	Method of Suicide
Women							
1.	22	1914	1936	S	2 yrs. college	S	Gunshot
2.	30	1905	1935	S	AB	A (librarian)	Carbon monoxide
3.	30	1913	1943	M	2 yrs. college	H	Gunshot
4.	32	1917	1949	W	3 yrs. college	A (physical therapist)	
5.	37	1916	1953	M[5],D[4]	2 yrs. college	A (writer)	Barbiturate
6.	40	1915	1955	M,D	3 yrs. college	H	Barbiturate
7.	44	1910	1954	M	MA	H	Barbiturate
8.	44	1910	1954	M,D	BS	A (social worker)	Barbiturate

*Occupational levels—Men: I. Professional; II. Official, managerial, and semiprofessional; III. Retail business, clerical, sales, skilled trades, and kindred; IV. Agricultural and related; V. Minor business, minor clerical, and semiskilled occupations. Occupational groupings—Women: A. Professional and semiprofessional; B. Business (includes secretarial and office work as well as work in other business fields); H. Housewife.

in Table 2. (The reader should keep in mind that all 30 subjects were male, Caucasian, Californian, middle- and upper-middle-class, had I.Q.'s over 140, and were members of the Terman Gifted Study.) Each folder was edited by Mrs. Oden so that I could not tell whether the individual was dead or still alive. (Death certificates, news-

Table 2

Occupations and ages for the suicide, natural death, and living subjects

	Suicide (N=5)	Natural (N=10)	Living (N=15)
Occupational Level			
I—Professional	2	5	7
II—Official, managerial, semiprofessional	2	4	6
III—Retail business, clerical and sales, skilled trades	1	1	2
Fathers' Occupational Level			
I—Professional	—	2	5
II—Official, managerial, semiprofessional	4	6	6
III—Retail business, clerical and sales, skilled trades	—	1	4
IV—Agricultural and related occupations	—	—	—
V—Minor business or clerical and semiskilled	1	1	—
Year of Birth			
1907	1	—	—
1908	—	—	—
1909	—	—	—
1910	1	1	3
1911	—	3	3
1912	1	1	4
1913	—	2	1
1914	—	3	3
1915	1	—	1
1916	1	—	—

paper clippings, and other "death clues" were removed.) The cases came to me, one at a time, in a random order. Although I was "blind" as to the suicide-natural death-living identity of each case, I did know the total numbers of cases in each subgroup.

Rating of Perturbation (The Life Chart)

T he cases were analyzed in terms of two basic continua (by which every life can be rated): perturbation and lethality. Perturbation refers to how upset (disturbed, agitated, sane-insane, discomposed) the individual is—rated, let's say, on a 1 to 9 scale*—and the latter to how likely it is that he will take his own life. (Lethality is discussed in the next section below.) For each of the 30 cases a rough chart of the individual's perturbation in early childhood, adolescence, high school, college, early marriage, and middle life was made. Clues were sought relating to tranquillity-disturbance, especially evidences of any *changes* and variations in the levels of perturbation. An attempt was made to classify the materials under such headings as "Early prodromata," "Failures," and "Signatures"—each explained below.

A "life chart" was constructed for each case, roughly following the procedures developed by Adolf Meyer (1951, 1952). In each case the folders were examined more or less chronologically in an attempt to order the materials in a temporal sequence while keeping in mind a number of related skeins.

One example of perturbation (from an individual who turned out to be among the five suicidal individuals): A high school counselor wrote about one young man that he was "emotionally unstable, a physical roamer and morally erratic, excellent to teachers

---

*The following point must be strongly emphasized: a basic assumption in this entire scheme is that an individual's orientations toward his cessation are biphasic; that is, any adult, at any given moment, has (a) more or less long-range, relatively chronic, pervasive, habitual, characterological orientations toward cessation as an integral part of his total psychological makeup (affecting his philosophy of life, need systems, aspirations, identification, conscious beliefs, etc.); and (b) is also capable of having acute, relatively short-lived, exacerbated, clinically sudden shifts of cessation orientation. Indeed, this is what is usually meant when one says that an individual has become "suicidal." It is therefore crucial in any complete assessment of an individual's orientation toward cessation to know both his habitual *and* his at-that-moment orientations toward cessation. (Failure to do this is one reason why previous efforts to relate "suicidal state" with psychological test results have been barren.)

who treat him as an adult but very disagreeable to others." At the same time, the home visitor wrote: "I like him tremendously; he is better company than many teachers." Ten years later the subject himself wrote: "My gifts, if there were any, seem to have been a flash in the pan."

Early Prodromata

Under this category were included early important interpersonal relationships, especially with the subject's father and mother. The folder materials contained ratings by the subject of his attitudes and interactions with each of his parents. Some information relating to relationships with parents may be of special interest. In the 1940 questionnaire materials—when the modal age of the male subjects was 29.8 years—there was a series of questions concerning earlier conflict and attachment to mother and father. The responses of the five individuals who, as it turned out, made up the homogeneous suicide group seemed to have three interesting features: (*a*) in answer to the question "Everything considered, which was your favorite parent—father, mother, had no favorite?" only one of the five answered "father"; (*b*) in answer to the question about the amount of conflict between the individual and his father and the individual and his mother, two of the five indicated moderate to severe conflict with the father, whereas none of the five indicated moderate or severe conflict with the mother; (*c*) the one suicide who was most obviously rejected by his father (and who indicated that he had had conflict with him) was the only one (of the five) to indicate that "there has been a person . . . who had had a profound influence on his life." He wrote: "My father, I think, has been responsible for a code of ethics stressing honesty and fair dealing in all relations." It was this man's father who insisted that he come into the family business and then called him stupid when he, for reasons of his own temperament, did not show the same amount of aptitude for business that his older brother demonstrated.

In general, for the five suicidal subjects, for reasons that are not completely clear, it seemed that the relationships with the father were more critical than the relationships with the mother. It may be that any exceptionally bright, handsome young child tends to be mother's darling and, for those same reasons, tends to be father's rival—hence the built-in psychological tendency for there to be more friction between father and son than between mother and son. (It all sounds vaguely familiar; I believe that there is a Greek play about this theme.)

In the perusal of the records, evidence of trauma or stress in early life was sought: the death of a parent, divorce of the parents, stress (either overt or subtle) between the parents, or rejection of the subject by either parent. In retrospect, I had in mind a continuum ranging from tranquil and benign at one end to stressful and traumatic at the other.

The folder materials indicated that at the time the study began practically all of the subjects were described in essentially positive terms. For example, among the five subjects who, as it turned out, were the five committed suicides, the following early descriptions by the home visitor appeared: "Attractive boy, well built, attractive features, charming." "Round chubby boy; very sweet face." "Winning little fellow, very fine all-around intelligence. The mother has excellent common sense and much is due to her." "Friendly, cheerful, freckled boy." "Tall for his age."

At the beginning, the psychological picture for most Terman youngsters was benign. However, in two of five committed suicide cases there were, at an early age, already subtle prodromal clues of things to come: "He is the constant companion of his father but he is not his father's favorite." (A few years later, at age 14, a teacher wrote about this child: "This boy's parents are of two minds; his mother is for college, his father thinks that college is of no value to a person who expects to take up the business. The boy does not show very much hardmindedness. His type is more the theoretical, he prefers ideas to matter.") During the same year, his mother wrote that the child's worst faults were "his lack of application and irresponsibility"—perhaps not too unusual at age 14.

Another example: A child is ranked by his mother as "average" in the following traits: prudence, self-confidence, optimism, permanence of mood, egotism, and truthfulness. We do not know, of course, how much of this is accurate perception or how much is self-fulfilling prophecy.

Still another example: At age 14 there is a series of letters from the head of his boarding school. (The parents were away on an extended trip.) The headmaster wrote letters having to do with the boy's veracity, perhaps revealing his own special emphases: "We have every hope of making him a straightforward young man. We are people he cannot bluff, and with consistent vigilance the boy will be able to overcome his difficulties." A few years later his mother wrote: "His success will depend a good deal on his associates."

Least Successful

In Melita Oden's (1968) monograph she presented a number of measures and comparisons between the 100 Terman subjects ranked as most successful and an equal number adjudged to be least successful. For each of the 30 cases that I have analyzed, I tried to make some judgment along a success-failure continuum. In the end, 8 cases were labeled as conspicuous successes and 5 cases as failures. As it turned out, none of those cases rated by me as "most successful" subsequently committed suicide, whereas 3 of the cases rated as "least successful" killed themselves.*

An example: a very bright young boy (I.Q. 180) who did very well in high school, both academically and in extracurricular activities. When he was 15 years old Professor Terman wrote of him: "I think there is no doubt that he would make a desirable student at Stanford." Within a year, at age 16, he had entered Stanford and flunked out. Eventually, after working as a clerk, he returned to college after one year and graduated. He earned a law degree going to an evening law school. He then became an attorney in a large law firm. He was described as unsocial and shy. In his forties he says he was inclined to drink rather heavily, but not sufficiently to interfere with his work. His wife is described as vivacious and he as withdrawn. After a heart attack, his income suddenly became half of what he had been earning. He described himself as much less interested than his peers in vocational advancement or financial gain.

Signatures

In each case I looked for some special (albeit negative) indicators that might in themselves, or in combination, be prodromatic to

---

*Among the 20 men who committed suicide, at least 3 were considered outstandingly successful by gifted group standards: 2 in the 1960 study and 1 who died in 1938 who had a brilliant record until his death at the age of 28. Conversely, 3 were considered least successful: 2 in 1940 (they had died before 1960) and 1 in the 1960 evaluation (Oden, 1968).

suicide. For example, alcoholism, homosexuality, suicide threats, conspicuous achievement instability, depression, neurasthenia, and dyspnea could be listed. All 5 of the committed suicides had one or more of these signatures items. An additional 8 (of the 30 cases) also had signature items. These items in themselves did not necessarily point to suicide, but when taken in combination with other features in the case they constituted an important aspect of the total prodromal picture.

Another example, this one emphasizing the lifelong instability of the individual: At age 7 his mother wrote that "he is inclined to take the line of least resistance." At the same time, the teacher rated him high in desire to excel, general intelligence, and originality; average in prudence, generosity, and desire to know; and low in willpower, optimism, and truthfulness. She indicated that, though he came from a good home, he was inclined to be moody and sulky. At age 8 his mother said he was strong-willed and liked to have his own way, that school was easy, and that he was making excellent grades. At age 10 his parents divorced. At age 12 the teacher reported that he was not a very good student and was doing only fair work, that he had rather lazy mental habits. At age 16 he graduated from high school with a C average. He did not attend college. In his twenties he became an artist. He was married. During World War II he was in the army. After the service he was unemployed and was described by his wife as "immature, unstable, irresponsible and extravagant." Because of his many affairs his wife, although stating she was fond of him, left him. She called him impulsive, romantic, and unstable. In his thirties he worked for a while as a commercial artist. He wrote to Professor Terman: "I am a lemon in your group." He indicated, as a joke, that his "hobby" was observing women from a bar stool. He remarried. He wrote to Professor Terman in relation to his art work that he "received much acclaim from those in the immediate audience," but that his works had not yet been displayed in any shows. His life was a series of ups and downs, some impulsive behaviors, and lifelong instability.

Apropos "up and downs" in general, any sudden *changes* in life status or life style can be looked upon as suspicious (i.e., prodromal to suicide), especially a change which marks a decline of status, position, or income. Generally, in suicide prevention work, one views any recent changes in life style as possible serious indicators of suicidal potential.

Rating of Lethality (The Psychological Autopsy)

I n addition to the life chart, the second procedure employed was one that I had some years before labeled "the psychological autopsy." This procedure is a retrospective reconstruction of an individual's life that focuses on lethality, that is, those features of his life that illuminate his intentions in relation to his own death, clues as to the type of death it was, the degree (if any) of his participation in his own death, and why the death occurred at that time. In general, the main function of the psychological autopsy is to help clarify deaths that are equivocal as to the *mode* of death—usually to help coroners and medical examiners decide if the death (which may be clear enough as to *cause* of death, e.g., asphyxiation due to drowning or barbiturate overdose) was of an accidental or suicidal mode. Clearly, the *psychological* autopsy focuses on the role of the decedent in his own demise.

In the last few years, a number of individuals have written on this topic: Litman and his colleagues (Litman, Curphey, Shneidman, Farberow, & Tabachnick, 1963) have presented a general overview of its clinical use; Curphey (1961) has written of the use of this procedure from the medicolegal viewpoint of a forensic pathologist; and Weisman and Kastenbaum (1968) have applied this procedure to study the terminal phase of life. Elsewhere (Shneidman, 1969b), I have indicated that three separate types (and uses) of the psychological autopsy can be discerned. Each is tied to answering a different primary question as follows: (*a*) why did the individual commit suicide? (*b*) why did the individual die at this time? and (*c*) what is the most accurate mode of death in this case? Given a death which is clear as to *cause* of death but which is equivocal as to *mode* of death, the purpose of this type of psychological autopsy is to clarify the situation so as to arrive at the most accurate or appropriate mode of death—what it "truly" was. This original use of the psychological autopsy grew out of the joint efforts of the Los Angeles County chief medical examiner-coroner (then Dr. Theodore J. Curphey) and the staff of the Los Angeles Suicide Prevention Center as an attempt to bring the skills of the behavioral sciences to bear relevantly on the problems of equivocal deaths. In those 10 percent of coroner's cases where the mode of death is questionable or equivocal, this equivocation usually lies between the modes of accident and suicide.

In the usual application of the psychological autopsy, the procedure is to interview close survivors (relatives and friends) of the decedent in order to reconstruct his role in his own death. In the present study, I was, of course, limited to an examination of folder materials.

All the criteria that have been discussed above—perturbation, including early prodromata, failure, and signatures—were combined into one judgment of that individual's lethality, that is, the probability of his committing suicide in the present or the immediate future. In this process of judgment I was guided by two additional governing concepts: (*a*) the key role of the significant other and (*b*) the concept of a partial death (or chronic suicide or "burned-out" life).

The Crucial Role of the Significant Order

In an adult who is suicide prone, the behavior of the significant other, specifically the wife, seems either lifesaving or suicidogenic. My reading of the cases led me to feel that the wife could be the difference between life and death. In general, a wife who was hostile, independent, competitive, or nonsupporting of her husband who had some of the suicidal prodromata seemed to doom him to a suicidal outcome, whereas a wife who was helpful, emotionally supportive, and actively ancillary seemed to save a man who, in my clinical judgment at least, might otherwise have killed himself.

To the extent that these global clinical impressions of the important role of the spouse, in some cases, are correct, then, in those cases, there is an equal implication for suicide prevention, specifically that one must deal actively with the significant other. A regimen of therapy or a program of education must not fail to include the spouse; indeed it might be focused primarily on the wife and only secondarily on the potential suicide himself. Of course, the conscious and unconscious attitudes of the wife toward her husband must be carefully assessed. In a situation where the wife is deeply competitive (and might unconsciously wish him dead), using her as an auxiliary therapist would at best be an uphill climb. It is possible that in some cases a separation might be a lifesaving suggestion. All the above is not to impugn the wife; rather it is to involve her appropriately. It could very well be that, had the study focused on female suicides, the above prescription would be in relation to the complementary role of the husband.

The Concept of a Partial Death

This concept is well known in suicidology. In the technical literature it was given its most well known presentation by Karl Menninger (1938) in *Man against Himself.* On valid psychological grounds it denies the dichotomous nature of psychological death and asserts that there are some lives that are moieties and only partial existences. Henry Murray (1967) expands this theme in his paper "Dead to the World":

> When I chose the phrase "dead to the world," I was thinking of a variety of somewhat similar psychic states characterized by a marked diminution or near-cessation of affect involving both hemispheres of concern, the inner and the outer world. Here it is as if the person's primal springs of vitality had dried up, as if he were empty or hollow at the very core of his being. There is a striking absence of anything but the most perfunctory and superficial social interactions; output as well as intake is at a minimum. . . . I have been talking about a diminution or cessation of feeling, one component of consciousness, on the assumption that this condition is somewhat analogous to a cessation of the whole of consciousness. If the cessation of feeling is temporary it resembles sleep; if it is permanent (a virtual atrophy of emotional life) it resembles death, the condition of the brain and body after the home fires of metabolism in the cortex have gone out. In a feelingless state the home fires are still burning but without glow or warmth.

That last statement about the home fires burning led me to think of a "burned-out" person—a person whose whole life was a kind of chronic suicide, a living death, a life without ambition and seemingly without purpose.

In the lethality ratings of the 30 cases, those that gave me the greatest difficulty were the chronic, nonachieving, "partial death" lives. I decided that I would rate this type of person among the first 12 in lethality, but not among the first 5. I did this with the conviction that this very style of living was in itself a kind of substitute for overt suicide; that in these cases, the *raison d'être* for committing overt suicide was absent, in that the truncated life itself was the significant inimical act (Shneidman, 1963).

Results of Blind Clinical Analyses

On the day that I completed the blind analysis of the 30th case I

wrote a memorandum to Professor Sears that included the following:

> My analysis of the data and possibly the data themselves do not
> permit me to state with anything like full confidence which 5
> cases were suicidal. The best that I can do—from my subjective
> ratings of each individual's perturbation and lethality—is
> to rank order 11 of the 30 cases as the likely candidates for
> suicidal status. I should be somewhat surprised if any of the
> other 19 individuals committed suicide. The rank order for
> suicide potential is as follows . . .

Then we—Mrs. Oden, Mrs. Buckholtz, and I—met to "break the
key."

The facts revealed that the individual whom I had ranked as
number 1 had, in fact, committed suicide, my number 2 had
committed suicide, number 3 was living, number 4 had committed
suicide, number 5 had committed suicide, and number 6 had
committed suicide. Numbers 7 and 9 were living; numbers 8, 10,
and 11 had died natural deaths. For the statistical record, the
probability of choosing four or five of the five suicide cases correctly
by chance alone is 1 out of 1,131—significant at the .000884 level.
Obviously, the null hypothesis that there are no discernible prodromal clues to suicide, can be discarded with a fair degree of
confidence.

Table 3 presents a summary of the blind analysis data in terms of
a brief vignette, signature items, success-failure ratings, perturbation ratings, lethality ratings, and suicide probability ranking for
all 30 subjects. (The "Postscript" information was not available to
me when I made these ratings and was added to the chart after all
the other ratings and rankings had been made.)

Much of my analysis of these 30 cases was inferential, sometimes
even intuitive—which is to say that not every clue or cognitive
maneuver can be recovered, much less communicated. But for what
it is worth, I deeply believe that a number of experienced professional persons could have done as well. Indeed, I feel that the
volumes of information generated in the past 20 years by suicidologists furnish the working concepts and the background facts for
making precisely this kind of (potentially lifesaving) judgment
every day of the year in the practical clinical situation. Knowledge
of this sort is now an established part of the new discipline of
suicidology.

One striking result was that among those who committed suicide

Table 3

Blind Ratings and Outcomes for 30 Matched Male Terman Study Subjects

No.	Notable Characteristics	Signatures	Life Success	Perturbation	Lethality	Suicide Rank	Postscript
1	NP hospitalization; divorced; great perturbation; talks of suicide at 15 and 20	Suicide threats	C-	7-8	High	1	Committed suicide
2	Deaf; professional; low drive for worldly success	Nonachiever	C	3-4	Low	12+	Living
3	Flunked out of college; obtained LLB; shy; ups and downs; drop in income; alcohol	Alcohol; ups and downs	C	6-7	High	2	Committed suicide
4	Insurance man in heart attack rut	—	B	3-4	Low	12+	Died—heart
5	Ambitious bank officer	—	B	3-4	Low	12+	Died—cancer
6	Brilliant professor of medicine; textbook author; good life	—	A	1-2	Low	12+	Died—cancer
7	Set back at adolescence by home stresses; obese; no college aspirations; withdrawn; low-level job; underachiever; stabilized	Underachiever; stabilized	C-	6-7	?	11	Died—heart

Table 3 (Continued)

Blind Ratings and Outcomes for 30 Matched Male Terman Study Subjects

8	Physician; too high standards for people; tones down	—	B+	5-6	Low	12+	Died—heart
9	Hand-driving rancher; dominated by mother	—	B	5-6	Low	12+	Died—cancer
10	Stable geologist; steady life	—	A	1-2	Low	12+	Living
11	Lithographer; brilliant; no family back-up; underachiever	Underachiever	C	5-6	Low	12+	Living
12	Multimarried; emphysemic; inventor; ups and downs	Dyspnea; failure	C	6-7	High	4	Committed suicide
13	Scion of business fortune; straight success line; father helpful and supportive	—	A	4-5	Low	12+	Living
14	Quietly successful in own small business; tranquil life	—	B	3-4	Low	12+	Living
15	Had all advantages; did rather well but not superlatively	—	B	3-4	Low	12+	Living

16	Neurasthenic; esoteric mother; underachiever; chronic suicide	Depression; neurasthenia	C-	6-7	?	7	Living
17	Artist; unstable; flighty; impetuous; willful	Instability	B-	7-8	?	5	Committed suicide
18	Insurance man; stable life; interesting siblings	—	B	3-4	Low	12+	Living
19	Brilliant child and siblings; needed a father; stabilized by second wife	—	B	4-5	Low	12+	Living
20	Pleasant man; pleasant life; pleasant family; likes work	—	B	2-3	Low	12+	Living
21	Early genius; hiatus; never fully recovers; wife commits suicide	—	B	5-6	Mdn	12+	Died—heart
22	Shy, depressed artist; multiple illnesses; making it	Depression; ill	B	6-7	?	9	Living
23	Unhappy; forced into father's business; rejected by father; always second to sibling; 4 divorces; unstable; downhill; alone	Depression; instability	B+	7-8	?	6	Committed suicide

Table 3 (Continued)

Blind Ratings and Outcomes for 30 Matched Male Terman Study Subjects

24	Average school administrator; ordinary stresses	—	B	4-5	Low	12+	Living
25	Well-adjusted, stable attorney; great relationship with father; good life success	—	A	2-3	Low	12+	Living
26	Depressed engineer; hypomanic wife; his job holds him	Depression	B	6-7	Mdn+	8	Died—cancer
27	Scientist; brilliant beginning; wife drains him; good but not great	—	B+	3-4	Low	12+	Living
28	Engineer; overcame adolescent crisis and parents' divorce; good marriage; has grown steadily	—	B	4-5	Low	12+	Died—heart
29	Author; asthmatic; depressed; strong support from wife	Dyspnea; depression	A-	5-6	?	10	Died—cancer
30	Professional stormy life; alcoholic; competing wife	Alcohol; instability	B-	6-7	?	3	Living

in their fifties, the pattern of life consistent with this outcome seemed clearly discernible *by the time they were in their late twenties.* The data subsequent to age 30 served, in most cases, primarily to strengthen the impression of suicidal outcome that I had formulated at that point. Those relatively few cases in which this earlier impression was reversed in the thirties and forties had one or two specific noteworthy elements within them: (*a*) a psychologically supporting spouse or (*b*) a "burning-out" of the individual's drive and affect. In the latter cases, this condition of psychological aridity and successlessness seemed to be the price for continued life.

What were some of the main clinical impressions relating to adult suicide in this gifted male group? In the briefest possible vignette, my main overall clinical impression might be formulated in this way: the *father*, even in his absence, *starts* the life course to suicide; *school and work* (and the feelings of inferiority and chronic low-grade hopelessness) *exacerbate* it; and the *wife* can, in some cases, affect the *rescue* from it (or otherwise play a sustaining or even a precipitating role in it).

Among the five suicides in this group, three types of suicidal prodromata—relating to instability, trauma, and control—could be differentiated.

Instability

In general, suicide is more likely to occur in a life where there has been instability (rather than stability). As used here, instability is practically synonymous with perturbation.

Chronic instability

Evidence of chronic, long-term instability would include neuropsychiatric hospitalization, talk or threat of suicide, alcoholism, multiple divorces, and any unusually stressful psychodynamic background—even though these bits of evidence occurred in as few as one of the five cases. Examples: Mr. A: NP hospitalization, divorce, talk of suicide at 15 and at 20; Mr. B: unstable personality, divorced, flightly behavior, few stabilizing forces; Mr. C: unhappy man, rejected by father, always second-best, four marriages, highly perturbed.

Recent downhill course

A recent downhill change that occurs in a career marked by ups and downs, that is, a generally unstable life course, was characteristic of suicidal persons. Specifically, these changes include a marked sudden decrease in income, sudden acute alcoholism, a change in work, and divorce or separation, especially where the wife leaves the husband for another man. In general, a sudden, inexplicable change for the worse is a bad augury. This means that in an individual with an up and down history, the most recent bit of information can be singularly irrelevant, if not outright misleading. Examples: Mr. D: highly recommended for university, flunked out of college, went back to school, earned an LL.B. degree, shy, alcoholic, sudden drop in income, up and down course, does not "burn out"; Mr. E: inventor, multiple marriages, up and down course, severe emphysema. (N.B., dyspnea can be an especially incapacitating symptom and has been related to suicide in special ways [Farberow, McKelligott, Cohen, & Darbonne, 1966].)

Early childhood or adolescent trauma

Examples would include acute rejection by one or both parents, lack of family psychological support, and separation or divorce of the parents. A crisis in adolescence can turn a life toward lower achievement.

Adult trauma

This includes poor health, such as asthma, emphysema, severe neurosis, obesity, and multiple illnesses. Another major type of adult trauma relates to the spouse, either rejection by the wife for another man or being married to a hyperactive (and competing) wife, who has changed from the woman he married. Examples: Mr. F, a depressed engineer whose top security job in aerospace holds him together; and Mr. G, who has a complicated, hypomanic, and successful wife toward whom he is deeply ambivalent.

Outer controls

These are the compensations or stabilizing influences in individuals who, without these assets from other than within themselves, would be more perturbed than they are and might commit suicide. Examples: the stabilizing work of Mr. F, mentioned above; the stabilizing wife of asthmatic Mr. H, a woman who nurses him and keeps the world from inappropriately intruding upon him or exhausting him. She husbands his limited energies.

Inner controls

These inner controls are not the usual strengths or positive features or assets of personality or character. They are the negative inner controls of default. One such is what occurs in some individuals who are perturbed early in their lives, who, if they survive, stabilize or simmer down or "burn out" in their fifties or sixties.

Examples: Mr. J: He was psychologically traumatized during adolescence by home stresses. He has no hobbies, no college aspirations, is withdrawn, and works as a mechanic and caretaker.

Mr. K: Extremely high I.Q. He is neurasthenic, has a mother with esoteric tastes, experiences back and shoulder pains just like his father, and is unable to hold a job as a professional. He calls himself "an unsuccessful animal." He ends up working as a clerk in a large company. His stance is that—to use an example from Melville—of a contemporary Bartleby ("I prefer not to"), what Menninger (1938) has called a "chronic suicide," where the truncated life itself can be conceptualized as a partial death.

Discussion

Whereas the clinical challenge is to be intuitive, to display diagnostic acumen, and to manifest therapeutic skill, the scientific challenge is to state theory and to explicate facts in a replicable way. I feel obligated to address myself to the theoretical side of this issue.

I shall begin with low-level theory, that is, an explication of the specific items that guided my thinking in choosing the individuals whom I believed had committed suicide. Some 10 items were in my mind: (a) early (grammar school, adolescence, or college age) evidences of instability, including dishonesty; (b) rejection by the father; (c) multiple marriages; (d) alcoholism; (e) an unstable occupational history; (f) ups and downs in income; (g) a crippling physical disability, especially one involving dyspnea; (h) disappointment in the use of one's potential, that is, a disparity between aspiration and accomplishment; (i) any talk or hint of self-destruction; and (j) a competitive or self-absorbed spouse. In summary, this low-level theoretical explication states that a bright male Caucasian who committed suicide in his fifties was apt to be: rejected by his father, adolescently disturbed, multimarried, alcoholic, occasionally unsettled or unsuccessful, disappointed in himself and disappointing to others, unstable, lonely, and perturbed with a penchant for precipitous action.

At a somewhat deeper level, and thus more theoretical, are the elements of rejection, disparity between aspiration and accomplishment, instability, and perturbation. At a still deeper level (and even more theoretical) is the notion that the suicidal person is one who believes that he has not had his father's love and seeks it symbolically without success throughout his life, eventually hoping, magically, to gain it by a singular act of sacrifice or expiation. The most theoretical formulation might be stated as follows: those tragic men who committed suicide in their fifties did not have that internalized viable approving parental homunculus that—like a strong heart—seems necessary for a long life.

It is interesting to reflect that the five special suicidal persons of this study constituted an essentially nonpsychotic group. This assertion is not to gainsay that each of them was severely perturbed at the time of the suicide, but they were not "crazy"; that is, they did not manifest the classical hallmarks of psychosis such as hallucinations, delusions, dereistic thinking, and the like. Their perturbation took the form—prior to the over suicidal act—of alcoholism, other than one marriage (single, divorced, or multiple marriages), and chronic loneliness, occupational ups and downs, impetuosity and impulsivity, and inner (as well as overt) agitation. Although, as it is in most suicidal persons, one can suppose that their thought processes were circumscribed ("tunnel vision") and tended to be dichotomous ("either a happy life or death"), there was no direct evidence to indicate that they were psychotically bizarre or paleological (Shneidman, 1969).

As has been noted by Oden (1968), the "magic combination" for life success among the gifted is not a simple one. For suicide also the equation is a combination of obvious and subtle elements. Many factors, none of which alone seems to be sufficient, appear to coexist in a suicidal case. And, as in any equation, there are factors on both the positive (life-loving, biophilic, suicide-inhibiting) and the negative (death-loving, necrophilic, suicide-promoting) sides.

In the algebra of life and death the spouse may play an absolutely vital role, holding the spouse to life or, at the worst, stimulating or even provoking him to suicide. Every suicidologist knows that suicide is most often a two-person event, a dyadic occurrence, and for this reason, if no other, the management and prevention of suicide almost always has to involve the significant other. With high suicide risk gifted males, my impression is that the most important lifesaving task is not directly to the potentially suicidal person, but through the wife—especially in concert with the family physician.

Currently, there is a small number of retrospective studies seeking to establish some of the early precursors of suicide among special populations presumed to be intellectually superior, specifically physicians and university graduates. A few words about each.

Blachly and his colleagues (Blachly, Disher, & Roduner, 1968) have made an analysis of 249 suicides by physicians reported in the obituary columns of the *Journal of the American Medical Association* between May 1965 and November 1967. Deaths from suicide exceeded the combined deaths from automobile accidents, airplane crashes, drowning, and homicide. The mean age of the suicidal group was 49. Blachly and his associates mailed questionnaires to the next of kin (usually the widow); about 30 percent of the inquiries were returned, many with extensive comments. The suicide rate varied greatly among the medical specialties, ranging from a low of 10 per 100,000 among pediatricians to a high of 61 per 100,000 among psychiatrists. A resume of Blachly's main findings is presented in Table 4.

Paffenbarger and his associates (Paffenbarger & Asnes, 1966; Paffenbarger, King, & Wing, 1969) have completed analyses of over 50,000 medical and social histories (including physical and psychological evaluations) of former male students at the University of Pennsylvania and at Harvard covering a 34-year period from 1916 to 1950. Their original focus was on individuals who subsequently died of coronary heart disease. The data drew their attention to those who had committed suicide—whom they then compared with their nonsuicidal cohorts. The 4,000 known deaths included 225 suicide deaths. Their findings relative to suicide point to paternal deprivation through early loss or death of the father, loneliness and underjoining in college, dropping out of college, and feelings of rejection, self-consciousness, and failure during the college years.

Dr. Caroline Thomas (1969)—like Paffenbarger, a cardiologist—is studying the causes of death among 1,337 former medical students of the Johns Hopkins University School of Medicine from 1948 to 1964. Her present project—as did Paffenbarger's—began as

Table 4

Summary of Findings of Three Studies of Precursors to Suicide among Intellectually Superior Subjects

Present Clinical Impressions*	Blachly's Tabular Results	Paffenbarger's Statistical Findings
a. early (before 20) evidences of instability, including dishonesty	a. mentally depressed or disturbed	a. college education of father
b. actual or felt rejection by the father	b. prior suicidal attempt or statement of suicidal intent	b. college education of mother
c. multiple marriages	c. heavy drinker or alcoholic	c. father professional
d. alcoholism	d. drug addiction or heavy drug user	d. father dead
e. an unstable occupational history	e. "inadequate" financial status	e. parents separated
f. ups and downs in income (not to mention ups and downs in mood)	f. death of close realtive in decedent's childhood	f. cigarette smoker in college
g. a crippling physical disability, especially one involving dyspnea	g. suicide of relative	g. attended boarding school

h. disappointment in the use of potential, i.e., a disparity between aspiration and accomplishment
i. any talk or hint of self-destruction
j. a competitive or self-absorbed spouse

h. seriously impaired physical health

h. college dropout
i. nonjoiner in college
j. allergies
k. underweight
l. self-assessed ill health
m. self-consciousness
n. subject to worries
o. feeling of being watched or talked about
p. insomnia
q. secretive-seclusiveness
r. "anxiety-depression" index (including nervousness, moodiness, exhaustion, etc.)

*Of course, not all of these features occurred in any one suicidal case; conversely, some of these features occurred in as few as one suicidal case. It was the "total impression" that counted most.

a study of the precursors of coronary heart disease but, in light of the data (14 suicides among the 31 premature deaths) shifted to include precursors of suicide.

What may be of especial interest in Table 4 are the common elements or threads in the findings of these three projects and the clinical findings of this present study. To what extent these findings relate only to the intellectually superior and to what extent they are universal is a matter for further study; nonetheless it is not premature to say that, on the basis of currently known data, it would appear that the common findings would seem to have general application.

References

Alvarez, W.C. *Minds That Came Back*. Philadelphia: Lippincott, 1961.

Binswanger, L. The Case of Ellen West. In R. May, E. Angel, & H.F. Ellenberger (Eds.), *Existence*. New York: Basic Books, 1958. Pp. 237-364.

Blachly, P.H., Disher, W., & Roduner, G. Suicide by Physicians. *Bulletin of Suicidology*. December 1968, 1-18.

Cavan, R.S. *Suicide*. Chicago: University of Chicago Press, 1928.

Cox, C.M. The Early Mental Traits of Three Hundred Geniuses. *Genetic Studies of Genius*. Vol. II. Stanford: Stanford University Press, 1926.

Curphey, T.J. The Role of the Social Scientist in the Medicolegal Certification of Death from Suicide. In N.L. Farberow & E.S. Shneidman (Eds.), *The Cry for Help*. New York: McGraw-Hill, 1961.

Dublin, L.I., Lotka, A.J., & Spiegelman, M. *Length of Life*. New York: Ronald Press, 1949.

Farberow, N.L., McKelligott, W., Cohen, S., & Darbonne, A. Suicide among Patients with Cardiorespiratory Illnesses. *Journal of the American Medical Association*, 1966, 195, 422-28.

Kobler, A.L., & Stotland, E. *The End of Hope*. New York: Free Press of Glencoe, 1964.

Litman, R.E., Curphey, T.J., Shneidman, E.S., Farberow, N.L., & Tabachnick, N.D. Investigations of Equivocal Suicides. *Journal of the American Medical Association*, 1963, 184, 924-39.

Menninger, K.A. *Man against Himself*. New York: Harcourt, Brace, 1938.

Meyer, A. The Life Chart and the Obligation of Specifying Positive Data in Psychopathological Diagnosis. Reprinted in E.E. Winters (Ed.), *The Collected Works of Adolf Meyer*. Vol. 3. Baltimore: Johns Hopkins Press, 1951. Pp. 52-56.

Meyer, A. Mental and Moral Health in a Constructive School Program. Reprinted in E.E. Winters (Ed.), *The Collected Works of Adolf Meyer*. Vol. 4. Baltimore: Johns Hopkins Press, 1952. Pp. 350-70.

Murray, H.A. Dead to the World: The Passions of Herman Melville. In E.S. Shneidman (Ed.), *Essays in Self-Destruction*. New York: Science House, 1967.

Oden, M.H. The Fulfillment of Promise: 40-year Follow-Up of the Terman Gifted Group. *Genetic Psychology Monographs*, 1968, 77, 3-93.

Paffenbarger, R.S., Jr., & Asnes, D.P. Chronic Disease in Former College Students. III. Precursors of Suicide in Early and Middle Life. *American Journal of Public Health*, 1966, 56, 1026-36.

Paffenbarger, R. S., Jr., King, S.H., & Wing, A.L. Chronic Disease in Former College Students. IX. Characteristics in Youth that Predispose to Suicide and Accidental Death in Later Life. *American Journal of Public Health*, 1969, 59, 900-908.

Shneidman, E.S. Orientations toward Death: A Vital Aspect of the Study of Lives. In R.W. White (Ed.), *The Study of Lives*. New York: Atherton Press, 1963. Reprinted, with discussion, in *International Journal of Psychiatry*, 1966, 2, 167-200; and in Shneidman, E.S., Farberow, N.L., & Litman, R.E., *The Psychology of Suicide*. New York: Science House, 1970.

Shneidman, E.S. Logical Content Analysis: An Explication of Styles of "Concludifying." In G. Gerbner et al. (Eds.), *The Analysis of Communication Content*. New York: John Wiley & Sons, 1969.

Shneidman, E.S. Suicide, Lethality and the Psychological Autopsy. In E.S. Shneidman & M.J. Ortega (Eds.), *Aspects of Depression*. Boston: Little, Brown & Co., 1969.

Stone, A.A., & Onque, G.C. *Longitudinal Studies of Child Personality*. Cambridge: Harvard University Press, 1959.

Terman, L.M. *Genetic Studies of Genius: I. Mental and Physical Traits of a Thousand Gifted Children*. Stanford: Stanford University Press, 1925.

Terman, L.M. Psychological Approaches to the Biography of Genius. *Science*, October 4, 1940, 92, 293-301.

Terman, L.M., & Oden, M.H. *Genetic Studies of Genius: IV. The Gifted Child Grows Up*. Stanford: Stanford University Press, 1947.

Terman, L.M., & Oden, M.H. *Genetic Studies of Genius: V. The Gifted Child at Mid-Life*. Stanford: Stanford University Press, 1959.

Thomas C.B. Suicide among Us: Can We Learn to Prevent It? *Johns Hopkins Medical Journal*, 1969, 125, 276-85.

Weisman, A.D., & Kastenbaum, R. The Psychological Autopsy: A Study of the Terminal Phase of Life. *Community Mental Health Journal Monograph*, 1968, 4, 1-59.

The Logical Environment of Suicide

This presentation is concerned with the logical environment in realtion to suicide. . . . The logical environment, is that which we call a logic of suicide. It is based on a classification of the qualities of reasoning independent of the content, and is largely a classification of the kinds of errors in logic and the types of implicit premises which the individual makes.

What things can be said about the logical environment of suicidal individuals? As the result of my analysis of some of the cognitive processes implicit in the suicide notes (which I did by analyzing the Aristotelian syllogisms and fallacies implied in the genuine and simulated suicide notes), I arrived at a tentative schematization of three types of suicidal logic, each with its own psychological counterpart and each with its own implication for treatment. I call these three types: logical, paleological, and catalogical.

The *logical suicides* are typically individuals who are in physical pain. The process of their deductions (as seen in the syllogisms which are implicit in their suicide notes) far from being psychotic is quite acceptable according to the usual standards for valid Aristotelian reasoning. They commit neither deductive nor semantic fallacies. They betray no basic confusions concerning either the nature of the self or the nature of reality. The psychological label for this type is *surcease suicide*. They are individuals who desire surcease from pain, and reason, correctly, that death will give them this. From this formulation there are some implications for treatment, specifically that treatment would have to give relief from pain (perhaps through the use of analgesics, sedatives, or surgery) and would have to provide companionship by means of active milieu therapy such as clubs, activities, home placements, etc. The syllogism inferred from such a suicide note is as follows: "I hurt and desire freedom from this pain. If I am dead I will not have this

---

From *California's Health*, May 15, 1960, Vol. 17, No. 22, pp. 193-196.

pain. Therefore I shall kill myself and feel pain no longer." We may not condone the act but we cannot gainsay the logic of this reasoning.

The *paleological suicides* constitute the second type. These are individuals who are delusional and/or hallucinatory, that is, they show the traditional hallmarks of psychosis. In their reasoning they make deductive fallacies by violating the rules for making logical identities. Also, psychotics lose the distinction between themselves and objects in the external reality and thus confuse the self and reality. Our psychological label for this kind of suicide is *psychotic suicide*. Certainly, not all suicides are psychotic, but psychotics can be—because their communications are generally not understood—unpredictably suicidal. Treatment has to deal primarily with the psychosis and only subsequently with suicidal tendencies, if they remain. Treatment should include protecting the individual from his own psychotic impulses. An example of psychotic syllogistic reasoning might be: "Death is suffering. I am suffering. Therefore I must die." This constriction and rigidity of attention may be the psychological reflection of the difficulty that the emotionally disturbed person has in grasping other than what is immediately in his mind, and may in some ways be similar to what one sees in catatonia when an individual can be so absorbed in his thoughts that he can let a cigarette burn through his fingers without his being aware of it.

Whatever the formal characteristics of his logic, the psychotic is the least predictable of all suicides. When the psychotic patient expresses suicidal notions, he is a double-barreled risk. Anyone hearing such expressions should communicate them immediately within the immediate community. Not only may the psychotic respond to the injunctions of hallucinated voices to kill himself, but he is also in constant danger of taking his own life in order to expunge the unacceptable and evil aspects within himself that he finds intolerable. Further, the activating mechanism for this explosive mixture may depend on the hair trigger of a dereistic thought, an hallucinated command, or a fleeting affective state.

Logical and paleological suicide aside, it is on the third type of suicide, the *catalogical type*, that I wish to concentrate in this presentation. Here the reasoning is characterized not by deductive fallacies—errors in the form of the argument—but rather by semantic errors, wherein the error is dependent on the meanings of the terms occurring in the premises or conclusions. An example of a semantic fallacy is as follows: "Nothing is better than hard work. A small amount of effort is better than nothing. Therefore a small effort is better than hard work." Here the fallacy is not dependent upon the form of the argument but rather on the ambiguous meaning of the terms "nothing" and "better." Another example of a semantic fallacy, this time with suicidal content, is as follows: "If anybody kills himself, then he will get attention. I will kill myself. Therefore I will get attention." The fallacy is concealed in the concepts contained in the word "I," specifically the confusion is between the self as it is experienced by the individual himself, and the self as he feels himself thought of or experienced by others. Actually, this is not so much a fallacy in the words of the reasoning as it is a confusion about the self, fallacious identification. Hence I call it a psychosemantic fallacy—and it may well occur whenever an individual thinks about his death, inasmuch as an individual cannot really imagine his own complete cessation. Another semantic fallacy has to do with the nature of existence and the confusion of the real world—our only world—with a possible hereafter. We call the reasoning that involves these semantic fallacies *catalogic* because it is destructive. It is destructive not only in the sense that it destroys the rules for semantic clarity, but also in that it destroys the logician.

Catalogic is not only contaminated by semantic fallacies, but it has a second characteristic: the penchant toward dichotomous thinking. Dichotomies abound in thinking. There are a number of psychological phenomena which express themselves in terms of opposites: doubt vs. certainty, insecurity vs. security, passivity vs. aggression, expectation vs. satisfaction, hope vs. despair, dependence vs. emancipation, acceptance vs. rejection, chance vs. organization, sacred vs. profane love, right vs. wrong, good vs. bad, and most relevant for our discussion, life vs. death. To think dichotomously is to make happy adjustment difficult to achieve. It puts one in what Bateson and Jackson call a "double bind" position. It's all or none: if one is not perfect, then he is nothing. One "goes for broke" all the time; and it can be lethal. Consider: ordinarily if a person does not like some aspects of his life (like his job or his spouse or his general situation), he thinks of changing those aspects, but if an individual organizes his world dichotomously and if the topic of *life* is introduced into his consciousness, then he must, logically, think not of some other way of living, but of *death* as the alternative. The dichotomous thinker is an individual who, to paraphrase from *Hamlet*, is haunted by his own polarities.

The world is filled with dichotomies, paradoxes, contradictions, duplicities, inconsistencies, and "double binds." The essence of adjustment is to be able to view these apparently frustrating insoluble situations as what Fromm called existential dichotomies rather than—as the schizophrenics and semantic suicides do—as historical dichotomies. Existential dilemmas—like the researcher's choice between precision and relevance—are always with us, but we can get along with them and live with aspects of both horns of the apparent dilemma and soothe and harmonize and resolve them in this way. Adjustment therefore lies in the fundamental abilities to make subtle discriminations and distinctions, to wink at disparities, to sense what is appropriate at the moment, to understand what rules must be broken, and on occasion even to do what one thinks is right rather than to act on one's principles.

Under the category of *catalogical* suicide we have subsumed two psychological types: *semantic* suicide and *sociological* suicide. *Semantic* suicides are typically individuals in their 20's, 30's and 40's who feel helpless and confused emotionally and feel pessimistic about the possibilities of making meaningful interpersonal relationships. Their confusions in semantics and logic are "referred," like referred pain, from other root problems, primarily those of psychological identification. Treatment would focus on the possible non-dichotomous choices and on the concept of the self. The method of treatment would be psychotherapy in which one goal would be to have the individual establish a meaningful interpersonal relationship so that his search for a stable identification would not be barren.

The other kind of catalogical suicide, also marked by semantic confusions and dichotomous thinking, is the *sociological* suicide. These are individuals whose conscious cultural and religious beliefs, especially about the hereafter, permit them to view suicide not as death but rather as a transition to another life. Inasmuch as the beliefs concerning the concept of death in relation to the self play a primary role in the suicide, the treatment would have to clarify deeply entrenched religious and cultural beliefs and deal with the semantic implications of the concept of death for that individual. Thus one sees that there are aspects of the logical and psychological environment which facilitate the acceptance of erroneous premises and invalid conclusions, and which account for many individuals making tragic deductive leaps into oblivion.

Suicide Notes and Tragic Lives

There is probably no description of suicide that contains as much insight in as few words as that found in the opening paragraph of *Moby Dick*: "... a damp, drizzly November in my soul." In its essence, that is what most suicide is: a dreary and dismal wintry storm within the mind, where staying afloat or going under is the vital decision being debated. In about one fourth of these occasions where a suicide is going to be committed, the individual will write something about that debate. Those documents—suicide notes—have something of the fascination of a cobra: they catch our eyes, yet we are ever conscious that some serious threat may lurk in them.

Suicide notes are cryptic maps of ill-advised journeys. A suicide note, no matter how persuasive it seems within its own closed world, is not a model for conducting a life. When one examines suicide notes, one can only shudder to read these testimonials to tortuous life journeys that came to wrecked ends. They fascinate us for what they tell us about the human condition and what they warn us against in ourselves.

My own long-term sustained study of them is admittedly a somewhat arcane pursuit. It would be like someone's contemporary fascination with alchemy, phlogiston or the inheritance of acquired characteristics, or with the notion that the world is flat, or that the earth is the center of the universe, or the proof that Bacon really wrote Shakespeare's plays—all flawed ideas. The difference that may make my obsession with suicide notes seem legitimate is that I know that suicide notes—like the many schizophrenic diaries I have read—are flawed rutters. I have never read a suicide note that I would want to have written.

But what can we actually learn about suicide from suicide notes? In the last twenty-five years, my answers to this question have undergone some radical changes. I have held three different positions on the relationship of suicide notes to suicidal phenomena.

From *Voices of Death* (by Edwin Shneidman), 1980, pp. 41-76. Reprinted with permission of Harper and Row.

My original view on the value of suicide notes dates from that special day in 1949 when I unexpectedly came across several hundred suicide notes in the vaults of a coroner's office. Since then, almost without a flagging of interest, I have been fascinated with suicide notes as perhaps the best available way of understanding suicidal phenomena. I believed that it was possible to unlock the mysteries of suicidal phenomena by using suicide notes as the keys. When one addresses the question: "Why do people take this trip?" (i.e., commit suicide), one can reasonably look upon suicide notes as psychological sources and search them for clues as to how the tragic outcome of that life's voyage might have been averted. It would seem that suicide notes, written as they are in the very context of the suicidal act, often within a few minutes of the death-producing deed, would offer a special window into the thinking and the feeling of the act itself. In no other segment of human behavior is there such a close relationship of document to deed.

My subsequent counterreaction to that view was a (somewhat exaggerated) jump to an almost opposite position. In that position I believed that suicide notes, written as they were by individuals in a state of psychological constriction and of truncated and narrowed thinking, could hardly ever—by virtue of the state in which they were composed—be illuminating or even important psychological documents. Admittedly, that point of view had a touch of "overkill" in it.

I now believe that suicide notes, by themselves, are uniformly neither bountiful nor banal, but that they definitely can have a great deal of meaning under certain circumstances, specifically when they are put into the context of the detailed life history of the individual who both wrote the note and committed the act. In those instances—where we have both the suicide note and an extended life history—the note will then illuminate many aspects of the life history, and conversely, the life history can make many key words of the note come alive and take on special meanings that would otherwise have remained hidden or lost. My present view is thus an amalgamation of my two previous views.

To readers who know their philosophy, this process will remind them of the ideas of the German philosopher George Wilhelm Friedrich Hegel. Hegel believed that all thought and development of ideas proceeded in a certain way. Specifically, the process begins with an affirmation of an idea (which he called the "thesis"), then it gives way to its opposite (the "antithesis"), and then the two are united by a new idea which combines them (the "synthesis"). This process (which may take minutes or years or decades or centuries),

repeated over and over, endlessly, Hegel called the "dialectic."
(This idea influenced Friedrich Engels and Karl Marx in their
"dialectical materialism.") What has happened over the last quarter century in relation to my own thoughts about suicide notes has
unconsciously mirrored some aspects of this basic dialectical process and might be called a "dialectical suicidology."

T he findings of many previous investigations over the past
century—starting with Brierre de Boismont's systematic
study in 1856—have been extraordinarily diverse and
diffuse. As a whole, these studies of suicide notes tell us
that the suicidal person—specifically as compared with the nonsuicidal person—is likely to think in terms of dichotomous logic,
separating everything in his world into two mutually exclusive
categories (like perfect and nothing, life and death), and to be
constricted and focused in his thinking; to think in terms of
specific instructions (as opposed to broad or philosophic generalizations), writing to his survivors-to-be as though he were going to be
alive to supervise his wishes; to avoid intellectualizing (i.e., to avoid
thinking about how he is thinking), dealing more with raw feeling
than with rational thought; to be concerned with blaming, both
others (the expression of hostility) and oneself (the expression of
guilt or shame); and to be concerned with love—the various aspects,
nuances and shading of affection, affiliation, devotion and either
romantic or erotic love.

The figures vary as to the percentage of individuals who commit
suicide who also leave suicide notes, ranging from 15 percent to
over 30 percent. Who, among those who commit suicide, writes
suicide notes? Except for knowing that note writers and non-note
writers are essentially similar in terms of all the major demographic variables—age, race, sex, employment status, marital
status, physical condition, history of mental illness, place of suicide
and history of previous suicidal attempts—we know very little
about the psychology of suicide-note writing. The distinguished
suicidologist Erwin Stengel, in his scholarly book *Suicide and
Attempted Suicide*, said: "Whether the writers of suicide notes
differ in their attitudes from those who leave no notes behind, it is
impossible to say. Possibly they differ from the majority only in
being good correspondents." That sounds like as reasonable an
explanation as any.

Studies of suicide notes have dispelled at least one myth about suicide: that suicidal acts are uniformly motivated by a single formula. Of course, no one commits suicide who is not, in some way and to some heightened extent, intellectually or emotionally distraught, but these perturbations can take the form of the passions of unrequited love, intellectual self-assertion, shame and guilt related to disgrace, the wish to escape from the pain of insanity, the wish to spare loved ones from further anguish, and a sense of inner pride and autonomy connected to one's own fate and the manner of one's own death. All these psychological threads, and more, are found in suicide notes.

Suicidal acts are very complicated psychological events—never mind their social, sociological or anthropological components. "Just" from a psychological point of view, there are many underlying, resonating and sustaining causes (together with a multiplicity of precipitating events) that come together in each suicidal event—hate, love, shame, fear, self-abnegation, hopelessness, to mention a few. . . .

W e have raised the question: What can we learn from suicide notes? Obviously, they often contain a great deal of interesting descriptive material, particularly of emotional states. But are they the full and explicating documents that would satisfactorily "explain" a suicide? The fact that a dozen and a half research studies by a score of qualified investigators over the past twenty years have *not* produced the new, important breakthroughs of information that one could legitimately expect from that amount of effort raises questions about their usefulness.

Overall, one might say that suicide notes are relatively barren compared with what we had hoped to find in them. It seems as though we tend to confuse the drama of the suicidal situation with our own expectations that there be some dramatic psychodynamic insights in the communications written during the moments of that drama. But the fact remains that memorable (authenticated) words uttered *during* battle or *on* one's deathbed are rare. It seems to be true also of suicide notes. Understandably, however, we continue to hope that even an ordinary individual, standing on the brink of what man has always conceptualized as life's greatest adventure and mystery, ought to have some special message for the rest of us.

Western civilization has for centuries romanticized death; we tend to read with special reverence and awe *any* words, however banal, that are part of a death-oriented document.

Perhaps suicide notes, by themselves, cannot be what we wanted them to be—for the plain and simple reason that they are written by a person whose mind (by virtue of being suicidal) is usually tunneled, overfocused, constricted and narrowed on a single goal.

A tragically precise and insightful description of tunneling and constriction is contained in the verbalization (reported in Chapter 2) of the young woman who jumped from a balcony.

> ... I went into a terrible state. ... I was so desperate ... That's the *only* way to get away from it. The *only* way to lose consciousness. ... everything just got very dark all of a sudden, and *all* I could see was this balcony. Everything around it just *blacked out*. It was just like a *circle*. That was *all* I could see, just the balcony ... and I went over it. ... [Italics added.]

As we read these chilling words we can practically visualize the constriction of her mind's focus, almost as the diaphragm of a fine camera closes down to its essential linear circle. And while this is happening, the mind's lens is adjusting to sharpen the focus on but a single objective. The objective is escape, specifically escape from intolerable emotion. It is at that precise moment of maximum constriction and focus that the picture is snapped; it is at that same moment when, as it were, the mind snaps and the act occurs.

Several suicidologists and literary writers have commented on the role of constriction in suicide. Margarethe von Andics wrote a book about suicide (one hundred suicide attempts in Vienna in the 1940s) in which she emphasized the narrowing of the scope of consciousness that was characteristic of the suicidal state; Erwin Ringel, also of Vienna, has written extensively, since 1958, of what he calls the presuicidal syndrome, placing great emphasis on constriction.

The contemporary English poet, novelist and critic A. Alvarez, who wrote an excellent book on suicide, *The Savage God*, has described what he calls "the closed world of suicide" in the following way:

> Once a man decides to take his own life he enters a shut-off, impregnable but wholly convincing world ... where every detail fits and every incident reinforces his decision. ... Each of these deaths has its own inner logic and unrepeatable de-

spair. . . . [Suicide is] a terrible but utterly natural reaction to
the strained, narrow, unnatural necessities we sometimes create
for ourselves.

Boris Pasternak, the famous author, writing of the suicide of
several young Russian poets, has stated:

> A man who decides to commit suicide puts a full stop to his
> being, he turns his back on his past, he declares himself
> bankrupt and his memories to be unreal. They can no longer
> help or save him, he has put himself beyond their reach. The
> continuity of his inner life is broken, and his personality is at an
> end. And perhaps what finally makes him kill himself is not the
> firmness of his resolve but the unbearable quality of this
> anguish which belongs to no one, of this suffering in the
> absence of the sufferer, of this waiting which is empty because
> life is stopped and can no longer feel it.

Because this sense of constriction exists in the suicidal person, is
it any wonder that suicide notes, written at the very moment when
an individual has lost touch with his own past, are taken up with
minutiae and are in other ways relatively arid and psychologically
barren?

Thus we see the relative barrenness of many—but not all—
suicide notes can be psychologically explained. In order for a
person to kill himself, he has to be in a special state of mind, a state
of relatively fixed purposes (not to deny an ever-present ambivalence) and of relative constriction of the mind. It is a psychological
state that, while it permits (indeed, facilitates) suicide, obviously
militates against good insight or good communication. In other
words, that special state of mind necessary to perform the suicidal
deed is one which is essentially incompatible with an insightful
recitation of what was going on in one's mind that led to the act
itself. Suicide notes often seem like parodies of the postcards sent
home from the Grand Canyon, the catacombs or the pyramids—
essentially *pro forma*, not at all reflecting the grandeur of the scene
being described or the depth of human emotions that one might
expect to be engendered by the situation.

To state the case strongly: In order to commit suicide, one cannot
write a meaningful suicide note; conversely, if one could write a
meaningful note, one would not have to commit suicide. Or to put it
in another way: In almost every instance, one has to be relatively
intoxicated or drugged (by one's overpowering emotions and constricted logic and perception) in order to commit suicide, and it is

well nigh impossible to write a psychologically meaningful document when one is in this disordered state.

Suicide notes, *by themselves*, may not tell us everything we want
to know. Life is like a long letter and the suicide note is merely a
postscript to it and cannot, by itself, be expected to carry the burden
of substituting for the total document.

T here is a vital reciprocity between suicide notes and the
lives of which they are a part. This statement—my
current position—is the synthesis of my two previous
attitudes: the thesis that suicide notes by themselves are
uniformly bountiful; and the antithesis that suicide notes have to
be constricted and pedestrian documents. Suicide notes definitely
can have a great deal of meaning (and give a great deal of
information) when they are put *in the context* of the life history of
the individual who both wrote the note and committed the act. In
this situation—where we have *both* the suicide note *and* a *detailed*
life history—then the note will illuminate aspects of the life history,
and conversely, the life history can make many key words and
ideas in the suicide note come alive and take on special meanings
that would otherwise have remained hidden or lost. It is close to the
art of biography. . . .

Suicide notes, written, as they are, as part of the life that they
reflect, can have a great deal of meaning (and give us a great deal
of scientific and clinical information) when they are examined in
light of the details of the full life history of which they are the
penultimate act. By putting a suicide note within the context of the
life history of the individual (who both wrote the note and committed the act), one can find that many words, ideas, emotional
proclivites, styles of reaction, modes of thinking, etc., that characterized that life are reflected in the specific details of the suicide
note. And conversely, many words, phrases, ideas, passions, emphases, etc., contained in the suicide note are extensions of those
very same threads that had previously characterized the life.
Living or dying, a particular individual has a certain consistency,
a certain "unity thema," a certain "trademark," which he or she
will show in work style, in play style and in life style, whether
celebrating life in a poem of love or contemplating death in a note
of suicide.

There is a bizarre but fascinating and incredibly inventive novel,

The Dwarf, by the contemporary Swedish author Pär Lagerkvist—
winner of the 1951 Nobel Prize in literature—about an aberrant and
evil dwarf (in a medieval Italian prince's court), which, by sheer
coincidence, contains uncanny and tragic parallels to an actual
contemporary case that I know. Indeed, the gruesome similarities
(in what a sadistic monster can do to a sensitive child) between that
honored work of fiction and the actual case are so striking that I
have decided to present the two in tandem. My purpose is not to
focus on the monsters, but rather on their victims. First, let us read
some passages from the novel. It begins:

> I am twenty-six inches tall, shapely and well proportioned,
> my head perhaps a trifle too large. My hair is not black like the
> others', but reddish, very stiff and thick, drawn back from the
> temples and the broad but not especially lofty brow. My face is
> beardless, but otherwise just like that of other men. My eye-
> brows meet. My bodily strength is considerable, particularly if I
> am annoyed. When the wrestling match was arranged between
> Jehoshaphat and myself I forced him onto his back after twenty
> minutes and strangled him. Since then I have been the only
> dwarf at this court.

One of the several subplots in *The Dwarf* concerns the prince's
young daughter, Angelica. Here is an excerpt:

> There is a great difference between dwarfs and children.
> Because they are about the same size, people think that they are
> alike, and that they suit each other; but they do not. Dwarfs are
> set to play with children, forced to do so. It is nothing less than
> torture to use us dwarfs like that. But human beings know
> nothing about us.
> My masters have never forced me to play with Angelica, but
> she herself has done so. That infant, whom some people think
> so wonderful with her round blue eyes and her little pursed
> mouth, has tormented me almost more than anyone else at
> court.
> We visit her dolls which have to be fed and dressed, the rose
> garden where we have to play with the kitten. . . . She can sit
> and play with her kitten for ages and expect me to join in. She
> believes that I too am a child with a child's delight in every-
> thing. I! I delight in nothing.

And then the dwarf's revenge on the child:

> Once I crept into her room as she lay sleeping with her
> detestable kitten beside her in bed and cut off its head with my

dagger. Then I threw it into the dungheap beneath the castle
window. She was inconsolable when she saw that it was gone,
and when everybody said that of course it must be dead, she
sickened with an unknown fever and was ill for a long time, so
that I, thank goodness, did not have to see her.

And finally, the dwarf's ultimate revenge on Angelica when she
has grown up to be a young woman: He informs the prince, his
master, that Angelica is being visited by a lover, who is, of all
people, the scion of the prince's hated rival family. The prince is
furious.

> "Impossible!" he maintained. "Nobody can come into the
> town over the river, between the fortresses on both banks where
> archers keep watch night and day. It is absolutely unthink-
> able!" ...
> "Yes, it is unthinkable," I admitted ... but think if the crimi-
> nal had already slipped away! Or if both had fled! The horrible
> suspicion sent me flying over the courtyard as fast as my legs
> could carry me, and up the stairs to Angelica's door.
> I put my ear against it. No sound within! Had they fled? I
> slipped inside and immediately recovered my composure. To my
> joy I saw them sleeping side by side in her bed, by the light of a
> little oil lamp that they had forgotten to extinguish.
> Now I heard the Prince and his men on the stairs, and
> presently he came in followed by two sentinels. Livid with
> wrath he snatched the sword from one of the sentinels and with
> a single blow severed Giovanni's head from his body. Angelica
> woke up and stared with wild dilated eyes as they dragged her
> gory lover from her couch and flung him on to the muckheap
> outside the window. Then she fell back in a swoon and did not
> recover consciousness as long as we remained in the room.

In the town there is a plague; Angelica suffers a rather peculiar
and different malady:

> Angelica cannot be sick of this plague. Her malady is the
> same as that which she once had as a child. I do not quite
> remember when, nor the exact circumstances. She has always
> been rather sickly, for reasons which could not possible affect
> anybody else's health. Ah, now I remember. It was when I cut
> off her kitten's head.

Finally, Angelica is driven to despair:

> Angelica has drowned herself in the river. She must have
> done it yesterday evening or last night, for nobody saw her. She

left a letter behind which leaves no doubt that she killed herself in that manner. Throughout the day they have been searching for her body, all the length of the river where it flows through the beleaguered city, but in vain. Like Giovanni's it must have been carried away by the tides.

There is a great to-do at the court. Everybody is upset and cannot realize that she is dead. I see nothing extraordinary about the letter, and it changes nothing—certainly not the crime which was committed and which everybody condemned unanimously. It contains nothing new.

I had to hear it again and again until I know it almost by heart. It runs something like this:

I do not want to stay with you any longer. You have been so kind to me, but I do not understand you. I do not understand how you could take my beloved away from me, my dear one who came so far from another country to tell me that there was a thing called love.

As soon as I met him, I knew why life had been so strangely difficult up to then.

Now I do not want to stay here, where he is not, but I shall follow him. I shall just lay myself down to rest on the river, and God will take me where I am to go.

You must not believe that I have taken my life, for I have only done as I was told. And I am not dead. I have gone to be joined forever to my beloved.

I forgive you with all my heart.

Angelica.

The Princess is convinced that she is the cause of Angelica's death. This is the first time I have ever known her to take any interest in her child. She scourges herself more than ever to efface this sin, eats nothing at all, and prays to the Crucified One for forgiveness.

The Crucified One does not answer.

Now let us turn to a real-life tragedy: the suicide of a twenty-three-year-old woman. I shall call her Dolores. This occurred in the 1970s, in a large city in the United States, in a motel room. She had brought with her a copy of Alvarez's *The Savage God* (in which he discusses the suicide of the poet Sylvia Plath). She registered under the name "Marilyn Plath." She hanged herself from the shower. She left this suicide note:

Forgive me. It was too late for me to be repaired. No one is to blame. I love you all. I want to be buried here. I am a broken doll. I have been to too many doll hospitals. They couldn't repair me. So dear doctor and Gregor, you were working against the impossible. How can a doll that has been through a mangler be repaired? I love you all for your great loving effort. Remember me with happiness for now I shall have no more pain.

Some few weeks before that eventful day, she had spontaneously written another personal document, a sort of essay of anguish, which she had entitled "What Is Depression?" Here it is, verbatim:

Depression is feeling revulsion from one's mother as a child. Depression is hoping to be the greatest love in someone's life and realizing it will never be so. Depression is knowing that although Maria, my nana as a child, loved me she went along all the way with the very strong mistress of the house, my charming mother, who constantly punished me for small reasons and instructed my nana to do the same. Depression is knowing that my family loved me but was told how bad I was, so love was limited. Depression is fear of having wanted to reach out to my mother and getting rejection in return. Depression is caring but beginning to stop reaching out. Depression is being a showpiece, the best dressed little girl. Who could say she hadn't the perfect mother? She dressed you so well—you have the nicest clothes—what a lucky girl you are to have such a wonderful mother. Depression is being noticed by my mother in public and ignored by her in private. Depression is knowing that I am being blackmailed by a little brother who knows he is the chosen one and having to do as he says. Depression is knowing that father loved me but never stood up for me—my mother was the master of the house. Depression is hearing over and over the story of my birth. The disappointment experienced by my mother of having had a girl. Depression is not really knowing if I was such an awful child—not being certain I couldn't have been such a revulsion without doing some great wrong. Depression is not remembering the wrong things. My father slept with a gun under his pillow—my mother told me I had access to it one day—that I pointed it at my mother and that it was taken away. I was about 3 and don't remember. *Depression was the killing of my dog and the murder of my doll by my brother.* [Italics added.] Depression is the development of hate, knowing that whatever I do I won't be loved. Depression was the encouragement of my parents telling my teacher to constantly punish me if I did anything incorrectly. Depression was being caned at school and beaten at home for having had to be caned at school. Depression is doing everything to be loved— but my mother saw to it that no one was going to love me. Depression is seeing love happening and suddenly disappearing. Depression is hearing that my brother makes my family so happy and I am a constant crown of thorns. Depression is my brother telling me that if I put sugar in my hands bees will make honey for me—Depression is being stung and having my mother laugh heartily for my brother's cleverness and my stupidity. Depression is hearing this hilarious story repeated over and over. Depression is the fright of being stung by a bee for the first time and wanting to be held and comforted and receiving laughter at my stupidity. Depression is knowing in life there is no real love—that love will die or the person will leave me.

There is so much more but I don't want to think anymore right now—but I hate her and all the people who couldn't love me just for me. They would just begin to love me and then meet her and the love for me would stop almost immediately. I am never going to let her take anyone from me again. I will do anything however wrong to prevent this—however drastic. I will stop at nothing.

This remarkable psychological document is a painfully shrill cry of hate and hurt. It is the wail of the psychologically rejected child; the lament of the unfavorite sibling.

Dolores was born in a major city in South America. Her parents were well-to-do and sent her to a fancy school—where she was beaten. After she finished high school in her native country, she came to the United States, attended a large university and had a lover, named Gregor. He was a tender man and extremely solicitous of Dolores's feelings. For some months before she died she was in psychotherapy. The following is a summary of some of her early memories as related to me by her therapist:

When she was born, in the hospital, her mother refused to look at her because she was not a boy. Dolores knew this well because her mother reminded her of it again and again, but also because she was also told this by the nurse when she was old enough to remember. Her mother did not look at her until she brought her home and then she was taken care of by this nana. Dolores has distinct memories back to about the age of four. Those crucial memories were somewhere between four and six. The critical memory is that she had a doll. It was an ordinary doll, nothing very special about it, but she absolutely adored it. One day she couldn't find this doll. They lived in a large house which had a walled-in garden and wooden pickets all the way around the garden, and she couldn't find her beloved doll and went out and there she saw, on top of one of those pickets, just the head of her doll impaled on the fence. The rest of it her impish brother had destroyed. [The brother verified that memory to the therapist.] But her feeling was that he had killed her doll and she said that over and over.

There is another memory which goes back to that time. These memories were also verified by her brother. This other memory—which dates back to a very young age—is of her grandmother's house, which was apparently not too far away from their house. Across from her grandmother's house there was a cemetery. Dolores remembers going often to the cemetery when she was very despairing, having been punished by her mother. At the age of four of five she would go to the cemetery whenever there was a funeral and she would sit and watch the mourners and all the beautiful flowers and she would say to herself, Oh, I wish someone would love me enough to care. She remembers her feelings of rejection as early as that.

The skeins of death were woven into her life almost from the beginning. Could it be that she was responding to her mother's unconscious (or even conscious) messages that things would be better if she, Dolores, were dead? A miserable childhood and the subtle parental cruelties of a lifetime can be a lethal potion.

When she was a young adult, her lover's concern and devotion could not pierce the impenetrable wall of Dolores's fixed feelings of being unlovable. In her distorted view of life, no one could give her enough love. Even her intense positive relationship with her psychotherapist was, not unexpectedly, contaminated with a fatal drop of deep childhood ambivalence.

The key imagery is that of the broken doll. The "broken doll" in the suicide note directly parallels the "murder of my doll" in the life history. In the same sense that the doll of her childhood was hopelessly destroyed and could never be repaired, she felt that neither could she—another broken doll that had been through life's mangler—be propped up enough to live.

Although there was no actual dwarf in her life, her mischievous little brother, encouraged by the mother, was the impish and sadistic figure in her childhood. Like the dwarf, he was a monster. There were also other symbolic monsters in her life (such as her unbearable feelings of rejection), which finally broke her delicate spirit.

We can begin to appreciate the reciprocal relationship between suicide notes and the lives themselves.

References

Edwin S. Shneidman, "Suicide Notes Reconsidered," *Psychiatry*, November 1973, Vol. 36, No. 11, pp. 379—394.
Margarethe von Andics, *Suicide and the Meaning of Life* (London: William Hodge & Co., 1947).

Erwin Ringel, "The Presuicidal Syndrome," *Suicide and Life-Threatening Behavior*, Fall 1976, Vol. 6, No. 3, pp. 131-149.

A. Alvarez, *The Savage God: A Study of Suicide*. (New York: Random House, 1972).

Boris Pasternak, *I Remember: Sketch for an Autobiography* (New York: Pantheon, 1959).

Selections from *The Dwarf* by Pär Lagerkvist, translated from the Swedish by Alexandra Dick. Copyright © 1945 by L.B. Fisher Publishing Corp. Renewed Copyright © 1973 by L.B. Fisher Publishing Corp. (now a division of Farrar, Straus & Giroux, Inc.).

Logical Content Analysis: An Explication of Styles of Concludifying

"... everybody conceives himself to be
proficient in the art of reasoning. ..."
Charles Sanders Peirce

"... we cannot call a man illogical for acting
on the basis of what he feels to be true."
Kenneth D. Burke

"Everything we do seems to be reasonable
... at the time we are doing it."
Donald Snygg and Arthur Combs

The purpose of this chapter is to suggest a method of analyzing certain aspects of an individual's cognitive styles and to relate these analyses to relevant aspects of his general personality functioning.

As a beginning, we assume that thought is a common characteristic of all humans (excluding neonates and unconscious persons). Each person does something that we call thinking, reasoning, cerebrating, deducing, inducing, syllogizing, coming to conclusions, inferring, and the like.

The most general term for these processes is "concludifying" (that is, coming to conclusions). It includes all of the mentational processes—cognitive maneuvers, logical gambits, sequences of associations, modes of induction, making deductive inferences—by which an individual can arrive at a firm or tentative conclusion.

Our second assumption is that individuals think in various *ways*, that is, that each individual has, along with his culturally common ways of thinking, some patterns of thinking that he may share with some other individuals and some that are unique to him. There is no one way of thinking, but there are many patterns of thinking.

From *The Analysis of Communication Content* (edited by George Gerbner *et al*), 1969, pp. 261-279. Reprinted with permission of John Wiley and Sons.

It has been asserted that there are modes of thinking that are peculiar to cultures (Whorf, 1956; Sapir, 1956; and Nakamura, 1960); we believe that, within each culture, there are also individual idiosyncratic patterns of thinking which, in their totality, are then characteristic of (presently unrecognized) groups of individuals within that culture. We recognize that two or more persons might reach different conclusions for reasons other than their different logical patterns—for example, by beginning with different premises or by difference selections and distortions of the evidence— but, in the present context, the focus of our interest is on the forms of thought (and the consequences created by nuances of difference in these forms) rather than on the premises or the contents of thought.

Each individual has, along with culturally common ways of concludifying, some ways of thinking that he shares with others in his particular culture and some that are absolutely idiosyncratic for him. Thus, ways of thinking (like other aspects of personality functioning) can be viewed in terms of the characteristics that are universal, ubiquitous, and unique. There is not one way of thinking, but there are many ways. In this chapter, we are not concerned with "correct" thinking or argument. People do not make mistakes in their apparent logic; there are good reasons for their seeming to be unreasonable. Thus, we are interested primarily in the processes of concludifying in which an individual thinker engages. By illuminating the characteristics of an individual's cognitive processes, we might then infer the psychological "reasons" (as well as his personality characteristics) which, for him, are consistent with his ways of reasoning. Notice that we are little concerned with the notion of "error" in reasoning. "Error" has generally implied a departure from a particular (theoretical) standard of thinking, usually that attributed to Aristotle when he was thinking about thinking. "Reasoning," to quote William James, "is always for a subjective interest." The "marriage" between an individual's patterns of thinking and other aspects of that individual's personality is binding whether "in sickness or in health." We are interested in how people *do* think, not in how they *ought* to think.

Our third assumption is that if one knew the idiosyncratic characteristics of an individual's cognitive processes, he would then be in a position to infer other facts about that individual, especially what that individual's view of causality and order are, as well as certain personality characteristics which are consistent with that individual's modes of reasoning. And, by virtue of this knowledge, he would be in a position to enhance (or to frustrate) communication with that individual.

In this approach to the logics of communication, there are four major categories of analysis: Idio-logic, Contra-logic, Psycho-logic, and Pedago-logic.

Idio-Logic

In this system, Idio-logic involves the individual's styles of thinking, referring to all those things that might be said—given the text of some original verbatim material (such as a political speech, a suicide note, or a psychological test protocol) by that person—about the syllogistic structure, the idiosyncrasies of either induction or deduction, the forms of the explicit or implied premises, and the gaps in reasoning or unwarranted conclusions, for example—indeed, anything that a logically oriented investigator who understood this approach could wring from a manuscript if he put his mind to it. These Idio-logical attributes are made up of two kinds of items: (1) *Aspects of Reasoning*, which include all categories that would traditionally be subsumed under "logical fallacies" (but that we do not view as fallacies but simply as idiosyncrasies), which relate essentially to the individual's inductive and deductive gambits and tactics; and (2) *Cognitive Maneuvers*, which describe the style of the development of thought, dealing especially with the flow of argumentation and with the cognitive interstices between the specific Aspects of Reasoning.

As indicated in Table 1, the Aspects of Reasoning are divided into these categories: (a) idiosyncrasies of relevance (for example, irrelevant premises, *argumentum ad populum*, false cause); (b) idiosyncrasies of meaning (for example, equivocation, indirect context, and the like); (c) enthymematic idiosyncrasies (for instance, contestable suppressed premises, suppressed conclusion); (d) idiosyncrasies of logical structure (isolated predicate and isolated term); and (e) idiosyncrasies of logical interrelations (for example, contradiction and truth-type confusion).

The Cognitive Maneuvers (Table 2) are divided into absolute statements (for example, to allege, to deny); qualified statements (to modify, to accept conditionally, and the like); initiating a new notion (for instance, to branch out, to interrupt, to digress); and continuing a previous notion (for example, to elaborate by phrase, to agree, to repeat).

Table 1

Aspects of Reasoning

	Kennedy (%)	Nixon (%)
Idiosyncrasies of Relevance Those features of the argumentative style invoking the intrusion of conceptual elements extraneous to the argument.		
A. *Irrelevant Premise.* Premise is irrelevant to the conclusion it is purportedly instrumental in establishing.	8.7	4.9
B. *Irrelevant Conclusion.* Conclusion is irrelevant to the major body of premises which purportedly establish it.	7.4	2.6
C. *Argumentum ad Baculum.* Appeal to force or fear in one or more premises where the conclusion in question does not involve these concepts.	1.7	.0
D. *Argumentum ad Hominen.* Appeal to real or alleged attributes of the person or agency from which a given assertion issued in attempting to establish the truth or falsity of that assertion.	.9	3.8
E. *Argumentum ad Misericordiam.* Appeal to pity for oneself or for an individual involved in the conclusion where such a sentiment is extraneous to the concepts incorporated in the conclusion.	.9	.4
F. *Argumentum ad Populum.* Appeal to already present attitudes of one's audience where such attitudes are extraneous to the concepts incorporated in the conclusion.	3.4	12.0
G. *Argumentum ad Verecundium.* Appeal to authority whose	1.7	.0

Table 1 (continued)

Aspects of Reasoning

	Kennedy (%)	Nixon (%)
assertions corroborate or establish the conclusion where no premises are asserted to the effect that the authority is dependable or sound.		
H. *False or Undeveloped Cause.* Falsely judging or implying a causal relationship to hold between two events.	1.3	3.7
J. *Complex Question.* A premise or conclusion of an argument contains a qualifying clause or phrase, the appropriateness or adequacy of which has not been established.	.0	1.9
K. *Derogation.* A premise or conclusion contains an implicit derogation of an individual or group, where the concepts expressing derogation are neither relevant nor substantiated.	.9	4.9
Idiosyncrasies of Meaning		
A. *Equivocation.* The use of a word or phrase which can be taken in either of two different senses.	6.6	2.2
B. *Amphiboly.* An unusual or clumsy grammatical structure obscuring the content of the assertion incorporating it.	4.8	3.0
C.1 *Complete Opposition.* The phrasing indicates an opposition or disjointedness of elements which are in fact opposed and disjointed.	2.6	.7
C.2 *Incomplete Opposition.* The phrasing indicates an opposition or disjointedness of elements which are in fact not opposed or disjointed.	—	—
D. *Indirect Context.* Indirect phrasing	—	—

Table 1 (continued)

Aspects of Reasoning

	Kennedy (%)	Nixon (%)
is used rather than direct phrasing in contexts where the latter is appropriate.		
E. *Mixed Modes.* An instance in which the context contains two or more of the following modes within the same context: descriptive, normative, or emotive-personal.	—	—

Enthymematic Idiosyncrasies
Argument contains suppressed premise or conclusion.

	Kennedy (%)	Nixon (%)
A. *Contestable Suppressed Premise.* A suppressed premise, necessary for rectifying initial validity of argument, is contestable.	5.2	3.7
B. *False Suppressed Premise.* A suppressed premise necessary for rectifying initial invalidity of argument is false, either logically or empirically.	2.6	3.0
C. *Plausible Suppressed Premise.* A suppressed premise necessary for rectifying initial invalidity of argument is plausible-but-not-obvious.	3.8	2.2
D. *Suppressed Conclusion.* The conclusion, while determined by the context of discussion, is never explicitly asserted, so that the point allegedly established by the argument is not brought clearly into focus.	.4	.7

Idiosyncrasies of Logical Structure

	Kennedy (%)	Nixon (%)
Isolated Predicate. A predicate occurs in a premise which occurs neither in the	42.0	41.6

Table 1 (continued)

Aspects of Reasoning

	Kennedy (%)	Nixon (%)
remaining premises nor in the conclusion, the function of such occurrence being to bind or relate the isolated predicate to other predicates, and *Isolated Term*: A predicate occurs in the conclusion which does not occur in the premise.		
Idiosyncrasies of Logical Interrelations		
A.1 *Truth-Type Confusion.* A confusion between unquestionable assertions on the one hand—logically true assertions and definitions—with empirical assertions on the other hand.	2.2	6.4
A.2 *Logical-Type Confusion.* Confusion between general and specific or between abstract and concrete.	—	—
B. *Contradiction.* Making conflicting or contradictory assertions.	.9	.7
C. *Identification of a Conditional Assertion with Its Antecedent.* Treating an assertion of the form "If A, then B" as equivalent to A.	.0	1.5
D. *Illicit Distribution of Negation.* Treating an assertion of the form "It is false that if A, then B" as equivalent to "If A, then it is false that B."	.9	.0
E. *Illicit Derivation of Normative from Descriptive.* To derive a normative statement from a descriptive, statement that is, a statement of the form, "It is necessary that X," "One should do X," "X ought to be," from ordinary descriptive statements, that is, statements containing no words expressing imperativeness.	2.2	.7
Total	100	100

Table 2

Cognitive Maneuvers

	Kennedy (%)	Nixon (%)
1a. To switch from a normative to a descriptive mode.	.3	.6
1b. To switch from a normative to an emotive or personal mode.	.3	.1
2a. To switch from a descriptive to a normative mode.	.1	1.0
2b. To switch from a descriptive to an emotive or personal mode.	6.6	5.2
3a. To switch from an emotive or personal mode to a descriptive one.	4.6	3.0
3b. To switch from an emotive or personal mode to a normative one.	.4	.6
5. To enlarge or elaborate the preceding, relevantly or irrelevantly.	7.9	6.0
7. To use an example, relevantly or irrelevantly.	2.3	2.7
8. To deduce or purport to deduce from the preceding.	2.8	3.4
9. To change emphasis, with continuity or warrant, or without continuity or warrant.	2.2	1.5
10. To make a distinction between two preceding notions, a preceding notion and a new notion, or between two new notions, with or without warrant, justification, relevance.	4.1	5.9
11. To branch out.	4.3	2.9
12.1. To synthesize or summarize.	4.1	3.0
14. To obscure or equivocate by phrasing or context.	6.9	4.6
16. To smuggle a debatable point into a context which is semantically alien to it.	5.8	8.4
17. To paraphrase or otherwise render as equivalent statements which, in	1.7	2.4

Table 2 (continued)

Cognitive Maneuvers

		Kennedy (%)	Nixon (%)
	general, are not to be taken as syntactically identical, with or without warrant.		
21.	To give a premise or assumption for a statement explicit or implicit in the preceding.	5.0	5.8
25.	To be irrelevant.	7.3	9.6
26.	To repeat or rephrase.	1.7	1.2
28.	To allege but not substantiate.	4.4	6.3
31.	To deny or reject with or without warrant.	2.8	2.7
35.	To agree with the whole but take issue with a part, implicitly or explicitly.	1.0	1.3
37.	To shift focus from subject to audience.	.0	.0
39.	To accept conditionally.	2.9	1.6
41.	To render another's assertion stronger or weaker by paraphrase.	.3	2.0
42.	To digress.	.4	1.3
42.1.	To initiate discontinuities.	4.3	2.0
43.	To resolve discontinuities.	.0	.0
44.	To perpetuate or aggravate discontinuities.	1.5	.4
46.	To go toward greater specificity.	4.8	5.8
47.	To go toward greater generality.	1.4	.7
48.	To transfer or attempt to transfer authority or responsibility.	1.5	.9
50.	To attack.	3.4	3.8
53.	To introduce a new notion.	.0	.0
54.	Others (of less than 1% each)	2.9	2.9
	Total percentage	100	100
	Total number of units	725	678

Together, these Aspects of Reasoning and Cognitive Maneuvers represent an attempt to explicate all the idiosyncracies of concludifying that an individual might manifest in his flow of thought. It seemed obvious that this general approach could be exemplified in an analysis of aberrant or "error-filled" materials. Studies of suicidal individuals and of psychiatric patients (Shneidman, 1961a) support this contention. The fact that this approach was also applicable to the study of well-functioning individuals was demonstrated by a logical analysis of the Kennedy-Nixon "Great Debates" of 1960 (Shneidman, 1963), if not by an analysis of a small group of Harvard undergraduates.

The numerals, listed on Tables 1 and 2 are the percentages taken from a detailed analysis of the first two (of the four) 1960 Kennedy-Nixon debate sessions. In this context, they only demonstrate that the distributions of the Aspects of Reasoning and the Cognitive Maneuvers of these two specific individuals were sufficiently different to distinguish them from each other, and further, to identify the separate logical styles of each. It was evident that Kennedy and Nixon were concludifying in very different ways; that is, independent of the *content* of their thoughts or the issues they were discussing, each would *process* the issue through his mind in ways quite different from the other. Given any tissue, each would tend to cerebrate it in his own way and, perforce, come to *somewhat* different conclusions.

By way of illustration, consider the following genuine suicide note, written by a 23 year old Caucasian Protestant female just before her self-inflicted gun-shot death—where the notations above the content of the note refer to the headings in Table 1 and 2:

Dear Folks:
    II-D   II-D   I-F   II-C1   I-F, II-D
I know this won't seem the right thing to you but from where I stand it
    II-D   I-F, I-J   39   II-A, II-B, I-J
seems like the best solution, considering what is inevitably in store for the

future.
    46   10   II-C1
You know I am in debt. Probably not deeply compared to a lot of people
    I-E   10
but at least they have certain abilities, a skill or trade, or talents with
                                       I-E
which to make a financial recovery. Yes, I am still working but only "by
I-F
the grace of the gods." You know how I feel about working where there are
                                             II-D
a lot of girls I never could stand their cattiness and I couldn't hope to be

lucky enough again to find work where I had my own office & still have
47
someone to rely on like Betty. And above all, most jobs don't pay as well as
7
this one for comparable work. I get so tired, at typing for instance, that I

couldn't hold a straight typist position. I wish I had the social position &
I-F   I-H
"know how" to keep this job. That way I wouldn't worry myself into such a
46
dither that I make stupid errors. Sometimes they're just from trying too

hard to turn out a perfect copy to please someone. With 3 separate offices

served by one board its pretty hard to locate people for their calls. And

when I do find them they don't want to take them—for which I really can't
I-H, II-B   II-c2
blame them as some of them are asinine. But when calls come in on the

board I have to dispatch them one way or another & the fellows don't
II-D
seem to realize that.
I-A
Some girls can talk about their work to their girlfriends and make it sound
II-c1   II-D   42
humorous but I guess it sounds like complaining the way I talk. And when

I mention anything to Betty, either in fun or in an effort to correct a
42.1
situation, it gets all over the office like wildfire. Now, when I sit there

paying attention to the board or my work the fellows think I'm purposely
9, II-c2   I-H
unfriendly. But just what is there to talk about when you get tired of the

same old questions & comments on the weather, "how are you," "working

hard or hardly working?" & you know better than to say very much about

things they're interested in or concerned about. I've usually tried to either
I-K
kid the person concerned about whatever it is or just shut up about it

because if one goes about telling the other persons business that can cause
II-c2
trouble. However, the kidding, or even a friendly interest, sometimes, can

hurt. So where are you? Might just as say very little and appear uncoop-

erative or whatever they think.

12.1   II-A, I-J, I-H
Due to these & many, many more frustrations from the board & other
                                                      I-D
causes I have become much more nervous than I was. You know what the

medicine I was taking did to me so far as my being extremely keyed up,

irritable, etc. was concerned. Now I feel just about as depressed as I was

keyed up then. I couldn't even talk coherently at times, and now I'm too
            I-H   42
concerned about my financial affairs to know what it is safe to say. How I
            I-F   I-F   II-c2
wish I could make "small talk" or "party chatter" like some girls do. But I

can't compete with most of them for many reasons & after trying to enter

into social activities with kids in my age range, especially the past year, I
                                    28
find that I can't compete with most of them. Even if I had all the clothes to
                                              42.1
look the part I still wouldn't be able to act the part. Sorry I'm such a

disappointment to you folks.
            I-H   I-A
I'm saying these things so you'll understand why it's so futile for me to
                        47
even hope for a better job. And as long as I go on living there will be

"working conditions" when there are so many other better places for the
            I-A, I-D
money. I don't mean to sound unappreciative of all you folks have done all
                                              10
thru the years to keep us kids well & healthy. It's just that I can't see the
            I-F, 7, I-J
sense in putting money into a losing game. I know I'm a psycho somatic—
            12.1
that's just it.
            II-A
One reason for doing this now is that Bill will be back & wants his .22.
 9
But the primary reason is one I think you already know—Mike. I love
                                    I-D   II-c2
him more than anyone knows & it may sound silly to you but I can't go on
            5
without him. What is there that worth living for without him?

  An analysis of the Idio-logic of this suicide note indicates that
there were 47 instances of 13 different aspects of reasoning and 27
instances of 15 different cognitive maneuvers. The aspects of

reasoning which appeared most frequently were I-F, Argumentum ad Populum, 8 instances; II-A, Equivocation, 5; and 2-D, Indirect Context, 9. For purposes of illustration within this chapter, I shall use but two of the aspects of reasoning: I-F, Argumentum ad Populum, and II-D, Indirect Context.

A brief explication of Argumentum ad Populum (I-F) is as follows.
Definition. Argumentum ad Populum is an appeal to affective dispositions and attributes of one's audience, where such dispositions and attitudes are extraneous to the concepts incorporated in the conclusion. The speaker attempts to influence his audience to accept his conclusion or position by citing certain real or alleged states which, while not part of the objective content of his conclusion, are consonant with an elicit certain "folk beliefs," attitudes, or appraisals held by his audience and, by their very familiarity, function to blunt any more critical or objective assessment of the speaker's conclusion or position.
Example. "I think that in common decency and common honesty, so long as the Senator from Utah knows what the obvious error is which has been deleted, he should tell the Senate" (*Congressional Record*, McCarthy, 1954/15849/2.9).
Discussion. The phrase, "in common decency and honesty," is used here as an emotional appeal to the body of Senators present—an appeal that is extraneous to the issue of whether the Senator from Utah has provided adequate grounds for his behavior.

Indirect Context—Aspect of Reasoning II-D—is defined as follows.
Definition. The speaker uses contexts of the form "I think that...," "It seems that...," "It looks like...," etc.—indirect contexts—as premises in an argument where the conclusion is in "direct" form, that is, is not relativized to appearances or beliefs, but is absolute. The speaker tends to relativize premises to himself (or to some other agency), while drawing conclusions which are not relativized. He weakens his premises to induce their acceptance and purports to derive a stronger conclusion than logically follows. He conceives of statements of the form, say, "I think that P" as logically equivalent to statements of the form "P" and uses the relativized statements in places where the non-relativized or "direct" form is logically required or contextually more appropriate.
Discussion. The preface, "I think that ..." relativizes the above assertion to the speaker. For instance, if we take the "direct" part of

the above, that is, the part starting with "in common decency...,"
then the appropriateness, plausibility, or truth of this latter assertion could be discussed by sociologists, legal philosophers, legal
scholars, ministers, etc., while the entire quoted assertion McCarthy makes, framed in indirect discourse, could be discussed only by
a lie detection expert or McCarthy's closest confidants.

The final construction of the individual's Idio-logic is essentially
an exercise in English exposition. One gives the greatest emphasis
to the aspects of reasoning which appear most often, or seem to be
"most important" in that subject's style of thinking.

One additional example: a very brief suicide note, "I love everybody but my darling wife has killed me." Its implied conclusion—in
light of the deed that followed it—is: Therefore, I kill myself. In this
short note one can detect two Idiosyncrasies of Reasoning: Equivocation (II-A) and False Suppressed Premise (III-B). The definition of
Equivocation is: A word or phrase is used which can be taken in
either of two different senses in a given context; or else in repeated
use of a word of phrase, the sense of the word or phrase changes;
the speaker does not fix the meaning of his terms; he leaves the
interpretation open; he does not give necessary elaboration to fix
unambiguously the meaning, or else he shifts from one meaning to
another.

In terms of that suicide note, the implied conclusion (Therefore, I
kill myself) is suppressed in the actual suicide note, but the note is
taken as giving grounds, rationale, premises, warrant, etc., for the
writer's taking his own life. The equivocation occurs with the word,
"kill," which in the premises has the sense of "violated," "be-
trayed," etc.—that is, "killed" in the figurative sense—while "kill"
in the conclusion is lethally literal in its meaning.

The definition of False Suppressed Premise is: A suppressed
premise, necessary for rectifying initial invalidity of an argument,
is false. The speaker tends to omit explicit mention of positions or
assumptions which are central to his exposition and which, more-
over, are almost totally idiosyncratic to him, being neither shared
by others nor independently defendable. In the case of the brief
suicide note, the false suppressed premises is: For any person X and
for any person Y, if X loves Y and Y kills X, then X kills X.

The following are examples—using actual suicide notes—of some
of the Cognitive Maneuvers:

To allege but not substantiate (to make an assertion, which is
nonobvious yet contextually important, whose context contains no

premise which would tend to establish it): "I cannot live any longer, I do not wish to live any longer. Death is better than living. Sometimes it is the best."

To deny or reject with or without warrant: ". . . and mother, I wish that you hadn't called me a liar, and said I was just like George, *as I am not.*"

To move toward greater generality: ". . . and about William, I want to dismiss every idea about him. I don't like him any more than a companion; for a while I thought I did, but no more—in fact, I am quite tired of him, as you know. *I get tired of everyone after a while.*"

To transfer authority of responsibility. (The speaker shifts to another person the responsibility for defending a position or handling a difficulty when it would appear incumbent upon the speaker to defend the position or eliminate the difficulty: "You alone know the answer. Your inhuman acts are the answer. Just search your mind and soul.")

To cite a premise belatedly: "Do not hesitate to tell any of our friends that I took this step of my own free will; I am not ashamed of it. *There is no reason why I should continue to suffer with no hope of recovery.*"

To repeat or rephrase: "I cannot live any longer. I do not wish to live any longer."

Contra-Logic

From the tabulations of an individual's Idio-logic, his Contra-logic—which represents his private epistemological and metaphysical view of the universe—may then be inferred. Under the assumption that there is a rationale behind each individual's reasoning, this procedure permits us to assert (or to estimate) what that rationale is, and thereby, to understand his reasons for his reasoning as he does. Contra-logic is our reconstruction of an individual's private, usually unarticulated notions of causality and purpose, which would make his Idio-logic seem errorless to him. The Contra-logic serves to nullify or contravene or "explain" that individual's Idio-logic and makes it sensible—for him. It answers the question: What must that person's beliefs about the nature of the universe be in order for him to manifest the styles of thinking that he does, that is, what are his underlying (and unverbalized) epistemological and metaphysical systems which are consistent with his ways of moving cognitively in the world? In the same sense that every person has an idio-logical structure which can be explicated, there is for each individual a complimentary contra-logical position which can be inferred.

An example will serve to clarify the concept of Contra-logic: A patient in a disturbed mental hospital ward—an example cited by Von Domarus (1944) and repeated by Arieti (1955)—unexpectedly says, "I am Switzerland." The reconstructed syllogism reads: I want to leave this locked ward—I love freedom; Switzerland loves freedom; (therefore) I am Switzerland. His Idio-logic is one of reasoning in terms of attributes of the predicate, but his style of reasoning would make "sense" to us (and does make sense to him) if it were the case (or if one supplied the implicit premise) that there were only one member to a class, that is, that Switzerland is the only entity that loves freedom. That is the Contra-logic which explains this Idio-logic, for in that case, it would follow without logical error that anyone who then loved freedom would, of necessity, have to be Switzerland. (The psychological concomitants of such a state are mentioned under Psycho-logic, below.)

Some other examples of Contra-logics, using a variety of kinds of individuals (a suicide, a Jekyll-and-Hyde homosexual, a chess champion, some noted political figures, etc.) are published in previous discussions of this method (Shneidman, 1957, 1961a, 1961b and 1963).

Let us continue our analysis of the suicide note from the 23-year old girl. The Contra-logic of Argumentum ad Populum is as follows.

Definition. It follows that one believes that: The acceptability or truth of a conclusion or position is not, and should not be, strictly a function of so-called "objective considerations," for any conclusion or position can be adequately assessed only in light of what the "going beliefs" and attitudes of the society are. Thus, the eliciting of these beliefs and attitudes be means of folk homilies, idioms, shibboleths, and the like is appropriate to assessment of the conclusion, that is, a conclusion is not independent of the whole nexus of societal beliefs, rather it is to be judged only in light of them, hence their elicitation is always appropriate. Truth is conventional and relative to society; it is not absolute or "extrasocietal." Concurrence of other men's views with the speaker's views is more important than concurrence of the speaker's views with the objective world.

The Contra-Logic of Indirect Context is as follows.

Definition. It follows that one believes that statements of the form "I think that P" are logically equivalent to statements of the form "P"; that is, indirect statements are logically on a par with direct statements. All knowledge is relative—relative to man, society, etc.—that is, to the perceiver or the asserter. There is no world or reality distant from our perceptions. There is no objective truth independent of, or in any way transcending, what any given man conjectures, surmises, and believes. A statement of the form "P" is to be understood as elliptical for "I think that P," that is, everything is indexed to the speaker.

We again examine the note from the suicidal girl, this time to see what can be said about her Contra-logic. Keeping in mind her use of Argumentum ad Populum and Indirect Context, the following might be said about her underlying idiosyncratic epistomological and metaphysical view of the universe:

There is no objective truth; what seems to be true for the observer is to be taken as true in fact (Indirect Context II-D). Validation of one's beliefs is obtained by concurrence of those beliefs with prevalent societal beliefs and attitudes, that is, one is correct in one's beliefs if others agree with them (Argumentum ad Populum, I-F). Everything that one asserts is already implicit in one's beliefs; if someone disagrees with you, it is because his beliefs are different from your own (not because he may be reasoning differently) and there is nothing to negotiate (Complex Question, I-J). Everything is relative to underlying assumptions (Cognitive Maneuver 39, To Accept Conditionally).

Psycho-Logic

The concept of Psycho-logic refers to those overt and covert aspects of personality that are related to—reflective of, are of a piece with, grow out of, create, or participate with—the individual's styles of thinking. The Psycho-logic answers the question: What kind of person would he have to be (in relation to his mentational psychological traits) in order for him to have the view of the world that he does (Contra-logic) as manifested in his ways of thinking (Idio-logic)? The fact that an individual's ways of thinking and aspects of his personality (Psycho-logic) are synchronous should come as no surprise to any student of human nature.

What aspects of personality are included under the Psycho-logic? In the present context we can be interested only in those psychological aspects that are reflective of the individual's ways of thinking, that is, reflections of his mentational functionings. No claims as to the manifestations of characteristics in other-than-mentational areas of activity (such as physical, sexual, or social areas) can be made. Furthermore, it should be stated that only with the most severe reservations can one generalize from an individual's mentational behaviors in any one specific situation to his entire logical armamentarium.

To return to our "Switzerland" example of the man who (Idiologically) reasoned in terms of attributes of the predicate, and who (Contra-logically) assumed that there was only one member to a class: that type of reasoning (Psycho-logically) reflects a mental state in which the focus of attention is *narrowed* (in this case, to one attribute of a class) and/or the freedom to widen or broaden the boundaries of the focus of attention is rather rigidly fixed. In such a state one might expect to see some of the following characteristics or symptoms: intense concentration or conflict; withdrawal from others; oblivion to ordinary stimuli; hypesthesia—even catatonic behavior.

Keeping in mind the restrictions indicated above, a set of Mentational Psychological Traits—that is, those psychological traits which can easily be related to patterns of thinking—is proposed. These traits are indicated in Figure 1.

To return again to our 23-year-old, suicidal girl, a summary of the Psycho-logic for this girl might read: The subject is relativistic and fearful of commitment (Indirect Context, II-D); she is needful of approval from others and attempts to elicit that approval whenever possible (Argumentum ad Populum, I-F); she tends to be distrustful and, if opposed, is intractable and rigid (Complex Questions, I-J).

Pedago-Logic

The Pedago-logic (relating to the process of education or instruction or pedagogy) can be viewed as a possible practical application of this method. If the Idio-logic explicates an individual's styles of thinking, and the Contra-logic describes his underlying philosophy of the universe, and the Psycho-logic details his personality traits related to thinking, then the Pedago-logic is a prescription that permits us to modify the process of communication or instruction for that person so as to maximize his opportunities for learning. To use an anal-

Figure 1

Mentational Psychological Traits

A. *Scope* (or *Range*). Wide-ranged diverse, broad-scoped versus narrow-ranged, focused, specialized. Generally, the compass of foci of concern: large, medium, small.

A.1 Global, holistic, totality; molar, large units versus molecular, detailed, atomistic.

A.2 Combinatory, extrapolating, seeing implications versus concrete, unimaginative.

B. *Discreteness*. Dichotomous, binary, either-or versus continuous, neutralistic, both-and, n'chotomous.

C. *Flexibility*. Flexible, adaptable, mobile versus fixed, inflexible, firm, rigid.

D. *Certainty*. Dogmatic certainty, affirmation versus uncertainty, indecision, doubt, equivocation.

E. *Autism*. Good reality orientation, nonautistic versus poor reality orientation, projection of standards, autistic. Generally: realistic (certain), realistic (possible, probable), unrealistic (impossible).

F. *Creativity*. Creative, original; novel, new, versus conforming, commonplace, banal.

G. *Bias*. Objective, unprejudiced versus prejudiced, infusion of affect, subjective. Also: reductive (derogatory), neutral, elevative (laudatory).

H. *Consistency*. Consistent, reliable, predictable versus variable, unreliable, inconsistent, unpredictable, fluctuating.

I. *Accord*. Builds on past achievement, extends accepted positions, accepts present authorities, constructive versus contrary, iconoclastic, perverse, negative, naysayer, destructive.

J. *Organization*. Systematic, organized, methodical versus unsystematic, disorganized, unmethodical, loose, scattered, disjointed.

K. *Directiveness*. Goal-directed, planful, purposeful versus lacking in direction, planless, purposelessness. Generally: compulsive persistence, appropriate persistence, impersistence (abandoning goal).

L. *Activity*. Aggressive, involved, adventurous, assertive, taking initiative versus passive, acquiescent, receptive, detached, timid, letting happen (lethargic), not taking initiative.

Figure 1 (continued)

Mentational Psychological Traits

Generally: proactive (taking initiative), reactive, inactive (apathy).

M. *Spontaneity.* Spontaneous, uninhibited versus constructed inhibited, controlled.

N. *Precision.* Definite, precise, clear-cut versus indefinite, vague, amorphous.

O. *Pursuit.* Tenacious, perseverating, single-minded versus changeable, labile, easily diverted.

P. *Orientation.* Action or fact-oriented, practical, unreflective, extrinsic reward-oriented versus mentation-oriented, contemplative, theoretical, philosophic, intrinsic reward-oriented.

Q. *Awareness.* Awareness of own cognitive activity versus unawareness of own cognitive activity.

---

ogy: everyone who moves at all can be said to locomote, but individuals locomote in many various ways. In this sense, the Pedagologic provides a way of "limping along" with the individual; it is a custom-fitted prosthetic device intended to facilitate his potential for locomotion. In the usual learning situation, there are at least two major aspects present: the substantive (what is being taught), and process (the way in which the "what" is presented— the teacher's way or the textbook's way). Most of us adjust to the way of the text or the teacher, but our grasp of content would be even greater if the content were presented *our* way, in a textbook custom-made to reflect our styles of cognizing. A good military aide soon learns to tailor the briefings for his General to fit the General's ways of thinking; a master coach adapts his teachings to the styles of his star players, so that he can maximize their potentials for performance. The Pedago-logic is a prescription for maximizing (or minimizing) communication.

The "thrust" of the concept of the Pedago-logic is perhaps illustrated best by using an example involving individuals of limited intellectual capacity. We—Peter Tripodes and I—made a few visits to a state hospital for the mentally retarded where we recorded our conversations with a small number of below-normal young adults. We routinely asked questions intended to elicit some sort of concludifying responses, such as "Why do you think so?" in relation to such topics of interest as privileges, visiting hours, dances, work, and release from hospital. We then analyzed the kinds of Idio-logics displayed by our subjects. Our thought—based on the notion that there are different ways to conceptualize (and thus to teach) *subtraction*—was to construct a few (three or four) simple textbooks teaching subtraction in the logical styles "consistent" with the three or four main types of logical styles we found among these subjects. Our hypothesis was that learning (measured, for instance, by rate, level of difficulty, and retention) by use of these "tailor-made" texts would be superior to learning from any one set (including their present set) of textbooks, simply because in the latter case some of the students would have to try to adapt to a style of presentation not peculiarly their own.

Although we did not have the opportunity to complete this study, the thoughts that stimulated its initiation may help to clarify the concept of resonating to another's logical styles. This same principle ought to apply, with even greater usefulness perhaps, in the school situation, or with military, industrial, or governmental personnel, especially in briefing leaders at the topmost levels. [Conversely, if one were meeting an opponent in a debate or at a bargaining table or in an international arena, it would behoove one to know that individual's logical styles (as well as one's own) in order more effectively to counter and to out-maneuver him—to beat him with his own game].

A summary of the Pedago-logic of the 23 year old girl's suicide note might include the following: The subject will either agree with you immediately or disagree with you forever, requiring a feeling of commonality in underlying beliefs in order to communicate with you (Indirect Context, II-D). This feeling of commonality might be elicited by your suggesting that your own beliefs are commonly held by others (Argumentum ad Populum, I-F). In the absence of such a feeling of commonality, she will tend to be oblivious to anything you might say thereafter (Complex Question, I-J). A summary of the analysis of her logics is given in Figure 2.

Returning, finally, to our I-am-Switzerland friend, one might concentrate on widening his intellective blinders, for example to show him (if it were possible) that there were countries other than Switzerland that loved freedom (Denmark and Israel, for instance) and that there were other-than-countries, that is, people who loved

Figure 2

Aspect of Reasoning	Idio-logic	Contra-logic	Psycho-logic	Pedago-logic
Indirect Context (II-D)	Relativizes assertions to own or other's perceptions; concerned with the appearance of events rather than the events themselves	There is no world or reality distinct from perceptions. There is no objective truth; there is only conjecture, surmisal, belief, etc.	Relativistic; fearful of commitment, feels divorced from reality, alienated from others.	This individual will see no objective grounds for your assertions, but will regard them as idiosyncratic to your point of view or attitude.
Argumentum ad Populum (I-F)	Appeals to affective dispositions and attitudes by the use of idiomatic expressions.	Truth is conventional and relative to society; societal attitudes are important determinants of truth and appropriateness.	Insecure; needy of approval; opportunistic.	This individual will tend to be responsive to the emotional content in metaphors, slogans, idioms, etc., and any other devices which connote widespread acceptance of your position.

Figure 2 (continued)

Aspect of Reasoning	Idio-logic	Contra-logic	Psycho-logic	Pedago-logic
Complex Question (I-J)	Uses phrasings that "beg" some critical points at issue by assuming that these points have already been established.	A position or conclusion cannot be negotiated or established by argument or proof, but is already incorporated in all one's assertions.	Distrustful, rigid, intractable, refractory. Tends to be fatalistic and tenacious.	In communicating with this individual, be fully explicit in making your point or she will tend to ignore it, having made up her mind beforehand.

freedom (for instance, Jefferson, Lincoln, Paine, and LaFayette)—
to break through, at the least, the narrow notion of Switzerland =
freedom, and freedom = Switzerland. On the other hand, his very
rigidity and inflexibility might militate against his listening effectively to any argument not isomorphic with his own fixed beliefs. It
is interesting to contemplate his reaction to your responding to his
"I am Switzerland" with "I am Switzerland too," to which, if you
possessed (and held) the keys to his locked ward he might then say,
"No, you are really Germany." Using this kind of language, you
might then reply: "All right then, let's negotiate. At least, let's draw
up a nonaggression pact." But, obviously, the most meaningful as
well as the most direct response to his saying "I am Switzerland"
would be to say—with seeming irrelevance but with piercing
perspicacity: "I know that you want your freedom from this locked
ward, and we'll see what we can do, you and I." Then you would be
talking his logic and he would know that someone had truly
understood him.

Summary

As with any aspect of human personality, it is useful to
consider man's mentational styles, following Kluckhohn
and Murray (1953), in the tripartite terms of (a) which are
common to all men—universal; (b) which are present in
some men—ubiquitous; and (c) which are present in only one
man—unique. In this chapter we have indicated our belief that
what is *universal* about mentational styles is that every human
(perhaps, other than neonates and decorticated nonneonates)
engages in some forms of concludifying; what is *ubiquitous* about
mentation is that there is a finite number of general patterns
(combinations or styles) of logical behaviors (which can be conceptualized in terms of the relative frequencies and clusterings of
Idiosyncrasies of Reasoning and Cognitive Maneuvers); and what
is *unique* are the special nuances of patterning or styles or thought
that specially characterize any particular individual's logical style.

All of this is conceptualized in terms of a four-part scheme:

(a) Idio-logic—which explicates the details of a man's logical
styles.

(b) Contra-logic—which attempts to explain why his reasoning
seems reasonable to him (by citing what appear to be his underly-

ing philosophies of causal relations which would "explain" his logical style).

(c) Psycho-logic—which surmises which traits of human personality might well be found with (or are consistent with) the idiosyncratic logical styles and the underlying epistemology of that individual.

(d) Pedago-logic—which extrapolates from the other three conceptions and suggests what logical styles might be employed (by a teacher or mentor or aide) with an individual so as to communicate and teach (or, conversely, to frustrate and thwart) that individual most effectively.

The general approach is one of attempting, without prejudgment, to understand the net results of an individual's ways of thinking by examining, in terms of logical, epistemological, and selected psychological dimensions, what manner of mind it was from which those results had come.

References

Arieti, Silvano. *Interpretation of Schizophrenia.* New York: Robert Brunner, 1955. *Congressional Record*, McCarthy, 1954/15849/2.9)

Kluckhohn, Clyde, Henry A. Murray and David Schneider. *Personality in Nature, Society and Culture.* Second Edition. New York: Alfred A. Knopf, 1953.

Nakamura, Hajime. *The Ways of Thinking of Eastern Peoples.* Tokyo: Japanese Government Printing Bureau, 1960. (Available from Charles E. Tuttle Co., Rutland, Vermont).

Sapir, Edward. *Culture, Language and Personality.* Berkeley and Los Angeles: University of California Press, 1956.

Shneidman, Edwin S. "Psycho-Logic: A Personality Approach to Patterns of Thinking," in J. Kagan and G. Lessor (Eds.), *Contemporary Issues in Thematic Apperceptive Methods.* Springfield, Ill.: C.C. Thomas, 1961a.

Shneidman, Edwin S. "The Logic of El: A Psychological Approach to the Analysis of Test Data," *Journal of Projective Techniques*, 25: 390-403, 1961b.

Shneidman, Edwin S. "The Logic of Politics," in Leon Arons and Mark A. May (Eds.), *Television and Human Behavior.* New York: Appleton-Century-Crofts, 1963.

Von Domarus, E. "The Specific Law of Logic in Schizophrenia," in J.S. Kasanin (Ed.), *Language and Thought in Schizophrenia.* Berkeley and Los Angeles: University of California Press, 1944.

Whorf, Benjamin L. *Language, Thought and Reality.* New York: John Wiley and Sons, 1956.

The Psychological Autopsy

I t is probably best to begin by defining a psychological autopsy and its purposes, then to discuss some related theoretical background and ways of actually performing psychological autopsies. The words *psychological autopsy* themselves tell us that the procedure has to do with clarifying the nature of a death and that it focuses on the psychological aspects of the death. Two ideas, important to understanding the psychological autopsy, need to be discussed. The first is what I have called the NASH classification of deaths; the second is the idea of *equivocal* deaths.

From the beginning of this century (and with roots that can be clearly traced back to Elizabethan times), the certification and recordkeeping relating to deaths have implied that there are four *modes* of death. It needs to be said right away that the four modes of death have to be distinguished from the many *causes* of death listed in the current *International Classification of Diseases and Causes of Death* (World Health Organization 1957; National Center for Health Statistics 1967). The four modes of death are natural, accident, suicide, and homicide; the initial letters of each make up the acronym NASH. Thus, to speak of the NASH classification of death is to refer to these four traditional modes in which death is currently reported. Contemporary death certificates have a category which reads "Accident, suicide, homicide, or undetermined"; if none of these is checked, then a "natural" mode of death, as occurs in most cases, is implied.

It should be apparent that the cause of death stated on the certificate does not necessarily carry with it information as to the specific mode of death. For example, asphyxiation due to drowning in a swimming pool does not automatically communicate whether the decedent struggled and drowned (accident), entered the pool with the intention of drowning himself (suicide), or was held under water until he was drowned (homicide).

From *Guide to the Investigation and Reporting of Drug-Abuse Deaths* (edited by Louis A. Gottschalk *et al*), 1977, pp. 42-56. Reprinted with permission of the National Institute of Drug Abuse.

The Psychological Autopsy

It so happens that a considerable number of deaths—the estimate is between 5 and 20 percent of all deaths which need to be certified—are not clear as to the correct or appropriate mode. These unclear or uncertain deaths are called *equivocal* deaths. The ambiguity is usually between the modes of suicide or accident, although uncertainty can exist between any two or more of the four modes.

The main function of the psychological autopsy is to clarify an equivocal death and to arrive at the "correct" or accurate mode of that death. In essence, the psychological autopsy is nothing less than a thorough retrospective investigation of the *intention* of the decedent—that is, the decedent's intention relating to his being dead—where the information is obtained by interviewing individuals who knew the decedent's actions, behavior, and character well enough to report on them.

Drug-related deaths can be among the most equivocal as to the mode of death. Proper certification often necessitates knowledge of the victim over and beyond standard toxicological information, including such questions as what dosage was taken (related to the exact time of death and the time at which autopsy blood and tissue samples were taken); the decedent's weight and build; the decedent's long-term drug habits and known tolerances; the possible synergistics of other ingested materials, notably alcohol or the effects of certain combinations like hydromorphone (Dilaudid) and Methedrine; and the role of lethal action of drug overdoses, e.g., morphine sulfate (morphine) as opposed to the quicker acting diacetyl morphine (heroin). . . .

Purposes of the Psychological Autopsy

As long as deaths are classified solely in terms of the four NASH categories, it is immediately apparent that some deaths will, so to speak, fall between the cracks, and our familiar problem of equivocal death will continue to place obstacles in our path to understanding human beings and their dying. Many of these obstacles can be cleared away by reconstructing, primarily through interviews with the survivors, the role that the deceased played in hastening or effecting his own death. This procedure is called "psychological autopsy," and initially its main purpose was to clarify situations in which the mode of death was not immediately clear.

The origin of the psychological autopsy grew out of the frustration of the Los Angeles County Chief Medical Examiner-Coroner, Theodore J. Curphey, M.D., at the time of the reorganization of that office in 1958. Despite his efforts, which were combined with those of toxicologists and nonmedical investigators, he was faced with a number of drug deaths for which he was unable to certify the mode on the basis of collected evidence. As a result he invited Norman Farberow, Ph.D., and me, then Co-Directors of the Los Angeles Suicide Prevention Center, to assist him in a joint study of these equivocal cases, and it was this effort—a multidisciplinary approach involving behavioral scientists—which led to my coining the term "psychological autopsy." (Curphey 1961, 1967; Litman et al. 1963; Shneidman and Farberow 1961; Shneidman 1969, 1973).

In the last few years, especially with the interesting and valuable work of Litman et al. (1963), Weisman and Kastenbaum (1968), and Weisman (1974), the term "psychological autopsy" has come to have other, slightly different meanings. At present there are at least three distinct questions that the psychological autopsy can help to answer:

Why did the individual do it? When the mode of death is, by all reasonable measures, clear and unequivocal—suicide, for example—the psychological autopsy can serve to account for the reasons for the act or to discover what led to it. Why did Ernest Hemingway "have to" shoot himself (Hotchner 1966)? Why did former Secretary of Defense James Forrestal kill himself (Rogow 1963)? We can read a widow's explicit account of how she helped her husband, dying of cancer, cut open his veins in Lael Tucker Wertenbaker's *Death of a Man* (1957). Some people can understand such an act; others cannot. But even those who believe they understand cannot know whether their reasons are the same as those of the cancer victim or his wife. What were their reasons? In this type of psychological autopsy, as in the following type, the mode of death is clear, but the reasons for the manner of dying remain puzzling, even mysterious. The psychological autopsy is no less than a reconstruction of the motivations, philosophy, psychodynamics, and existential crises of the decedent.

How did the individual die, and when—that is, why at that particular time? When a death, usually a natural death, is protracted, the individual dying gradually over a period of time, the psychological autopsy helps to illumine the sociopsychological reasons why he died at that time. This type of psychological autopsy is illustrated by the following brief case from Weisman and Kastenbaum (1968):

An 85-year-old man had suffered with chronic bronchitis and
emphysema for many years but was alert and active otherwise.
He had eagerly anticipated going to his son's home for Thanksgiving and when the day arrived he was dressed and ready, but
no one came for him. He became more concerned as the hours
went by. He asked the nurse about messages, but there were
none, and he finally realized that he would have to spend the
holiday at the hospital. After this disappointment the patient
kept more and more to himself, offered little and accepted only
minimal care. Within a few weeks he was dead.

The implication here is that the patient's disappointment and his
resignation to it were not unrelated to his sudden downhill course
and his death soon afterward, i.e., if his son had come to take him
out for Thanksgiving, the old man would have lived considerably
longer than he did. This man's death like some others—voodoo
deaths, unexplained deaths under anesthesia, and "self-fulfilling
prophecy" deaths, for example—must be considered subintentioned. There can be little doubt that often some connection exists
between the psychology of the individual and the time of his death
(Shneidman 1963).

There is, of course, a wide spectrum of applicability of this
concept. When a person has been literally scared to death by his
belief in the power of voodoo, the role of the victim's psychological
state seems fairly obvious; and it is difficult to believe that there
was no psychological connection between the fatal stroke of Mrs.
Loree Bailey, owner of the Lorraine Motel in Memphis, and the
assassination of Martin Luther King, Jr., at the motel 3 hours
earlier. But in many other cases any relationship between the
individual's psychological state and the time of his death seems
difficult or impossible to establish.

As an example of the problems raised by this concept, consider
the following case, reported in the *New York Times* of June 26,
1968:

WIDOW, 104, DIES IN COTTAGE
SHE ENTERED AS 1887 BRIDE

Mrs. John Charles Dalrymple, 104 years old, died here [Ran-
dolph Township, N.J.] yesterday in the cottage to which she
came as a bride in 1887.

Her husband brought her in a sleigh to the house, which she
was to leave next week to make way for the new Morris County
Community College. . . .

The main question here, as in Weisman and Kastenbaum's case of the old man who was left alone on Thanksgiving, is: Might even this person have lived at least a little longer had she not suffered the psychologically traumatic threat of being dispossessed from the home where she had lived for 81 years? Or does the question in this particular case tax one's commonsense credulity?

What is the most probable mode of death? This was the question to which the psychological autopsy was initially addressed. When cause of death can be clearly established but mode of death is equivocal, the purpose of the psychological autopsy is to establish the mode of death with as great a degree of accuracy as possible. Here are three simplified examples:

Cause of death: asphyxiation due to drowning. A woman found in her swimming pool. Question as to correct mode: Did she "drown" (accident), or was it intentional (suicide)?

Cause of death: multiple crushing injuries. A man found dead at the foot of a tall building. Question as to correct mode: Did he fall (accident), jump (suicide), or was he pushed or thrown (homicide)?

Cause of death: barbiturate intoxication due to overdose. A woman found in her bed. Question as to correct mode: Would she be surprised to know that she was dead (accident), or is this what she had planned (suicide)?

The typical coroner's office, whether headed by a medical examiner or by a lay coroner, is more likely to be accurate in its certification of natural and accidental deaths than of those deaths that might be suicides. Curphey says, "A major reason for this, of course, is that both the pathologist and the lay investigator lack sufficient training in the field of human behavior to be able to estimate with any fair degree of accuracy the mental processes of the victim likely to lead to suicidal death. It is here that the social scientists, with their special skills in human behavior, can offer us much valuable assistance" (Curphey 1961).

The professional personnel who constitute a "death investigation team" obviously should hold no brief for one particular mode of death over any other. In essence, the members of the death investigation team interview persons who knew the deceased—and attempt to reconstruct his lifestyle, focusing particularly on the period just prior to his death. If the information they receive contains any clues pointing to suicide, their especially attuned ears will recognize them. They listen for any overt or covert communications that might illuminate the decedent's role (if any) in his own demise. They then make a reasoned extrapolation of the victim's intention and behavior over the days and minutes preceding his death, using all the information they have obtained.

Conducting the Psychological Autopsy

How is a psychological autopsy performed? It is done by talking to some key persons—spouse, lover, parent, grown child, friend, colleague, physician, supervisor, coworker—who knew the decedent. The "talking to" is done gently, a mixture of conversation, interview, emotional support, general questions, and a good deal of listening. I always telephone and then go out to the home. After rapport is established, a good general opening question might be: "Please tell me, what was he (she) like?" Sometimes clothes and material possessions are looked at, photographs shown, and even diaries and correspondence shared. (On one occasion, the widow showed me her late husband's suicide note which she had hidden from the police!— rather changing the equivocal nature of the death.)

In general, I do not have a fixed outline in mind while conducting a psychological autopsy, but, inasmuch as outlines have been requested from time to time, one is presented below with the dual cautions that it should not be followed slavishly and that the investigator should be ever mindful that he may be asking questions that are very painful to people in an obvious grief-laden situation. The person who conducts a psychological autopsy should participate, as far as he is genuinely able, in the anguish of the bereaved person and should always do his work with the mental health of the survivors in mind.

Here, then, are some categories that might be included in a psychological autopsy (Shneidman 1969):
1. Information identifying victim (name, age, address, marital status, religious practices, occupation, and other details)
2. Details of the death (including the cause or method and other pertinent details)
3. Brief outline of victim's history (siblings, marriage, medical illnesses, medical treatment, psychotherapy, suicide attempts)
4. Death history of victim's family (suicides, cancer, other fatal illnesses, ages at death, and other details)
5. Description of the personality and lifestyle of the victim

6. Victim's typical patterns of reaction to stress, emotional upsets, and periods of disequilibrium
7. Any recent—from last few days to last 12 months—upsets, pressures, tensions, or anticipations of trouble
8. Role of alcohol or drugs in (a) overall lifestyle of victim, and (b) his death
9. Nature of victim's interpersonal relationships (including those with physicians)
10. Fantasies, dreams, thoughts, premonitions, or fears of victim relating to death, accident, or suicide
11. Changes in the victim before death (of habits, hobbies, eating, sexual patterns, and other life routines)
12. Information relating to the "life side" of victim (upswings, successes, plans)
13. Assessment of intention, i.e., role of the victim in his own demise
14. Rating of lethality (described in the final section of this chapter)
15. Reaction of informants to victim's death
16. Comments, special features, etc.

In conducting the interviews during a psychological autopsy, it is often best to ask open-ended questions that permit the respondent to associate to relevant details without being made painfully aware of the specific interests of the questioner. As an example: I might be very interested in knowing whether or not there was a change (specifically, a recent sharp decline) in the decedent's eating habits. Rather than ask directly, "Did his appetite drop recently?" a question almost calculated to elicit a defensive response, I have asked a more general question such as, "Did he have any favorite foods?" Obviously, my interest is not to learn what foods he preferred. Not atypically, the respondent will tell me what the decedent's favorite foods were and then go on to talk about recent changes in his eating habits—"Nothing I fixed for him seemed to please him"—and even proceed to relate other recent changes, such as changing patterns in social or sexual or recreational habits, changes which diagnostically would seem to be related to a dysphoric person, not inconsistent with a suicidal or subintentioned death.

In relation to a barbiturate death* where the mode of death is

---

*I am grateful to Dr. Michael S. Backenheimer of the National Institute of Drug Abuse for the suggestions contained in this paragraph.

equivocal (between suicide and accident), it might be callous to ask the next of kin, "Did your husband (wife) have a history of taking barbiturates?" A more respectful and productive question might be, "Did he (she) take occasional medication to help him (her) sleep at night?" If the response to this question is in the affirmative, one might then ask if the respondent knows the name of the medication or even the shape and color of the medication. If one determines that the deceased in fact had a history of taking sleeping medication, one might then ask if the decedent was accustomed to having some occasional alcoholic beverages prior to going to sleep. If these facts can be brought into the open, it may well be that one can then establish the quantity of the medication and alcohol content that the decedent was taking immediately prior to his death. The general method of questioning is one of "successive approaches," wherein the respondent's willingness to answer one question gives permission to ask the next one. That is the general way that one would inquire, if it were relevant, into, say, drug patterns of behavior. Where suicide or homicide is a possible mode of death, it is rather important to know whether or not the decedent was "into" drugs, an habitual user, or a dealer, on what terms he was with his dealer, etc.

Functions of the Psychological Autopsy

The questions should be as detailed (and lines of inquiry pursued) only as they bear on clarifying the mode of death. All else would seem to be extraneous. And to do this depends, of course, on having established rapport with the respondent.

The results of these interviewing procedures are then discussed with the chief medical examiner or coroner. Because it is his responsibility to indicate (or amend) the mode of death, all available psychological information should be included in the total data at his disposal. Since a sizable percentage of deaths are equivocal as to mode precisely because these psychological factors are unknown, medical examiners and coroners throughout the country are robbing themselves of important information when they fail to employ the special skills of the behavioral scientists in cases of equivocal deaths. The skills of behavioral scientists should be employed in the same way as the skills of biochemists, toxicologists, histologists, pathologists, microscopists, and other physical scientists. The time has long since passed when we could enjoy the luxury of disregarding the basic teachings of 20th century psychodynamic psychology and psychiatry. Certification procedures (and the death certificates on which they are recorded) should reflect the role of the decedent in his own demise, and in equivocal cases this cannot be done without a psychological autopsy.

The retrospective analysis of deaths not only serves to increase the accuracy of certification (which is in the best interests of the overall mental health concerns of the community), but also has the heuristic function of providing the serious investigator with clues that he may then use to assess lethal intent in living persons.

And there is still another function that the psychological autopsy serves: In working with the bereaved survivors to elicit data relative to appropriate certification, a skillful and empathic investigator is able to conduct the interviews in such a way that they are of actual therapeutic value to the survivors. A psychological autopsy should never be conducted so that any aspect of it is iatrogenic. Commenting on this important mental health function of the psychological autopsy, Curphey (1961) has stated:

> The members of the death investigation team, because of their special skills, are alert in their interviews with survivors to evidences of extreme guilt, serious depression, and the need for special help in formulating plans for solving specific problems such as caring for children whose parents committed suicide. Since we noted this phenomenon, the coroner's office has, in some few cases, referred distraught survivors of suicide victims to members of the team specifically for supportive interviews even when the suicidal mode of death was not in doubt.

This therapeutic work with the survivor-victims of a dire event is called *postvention* and has been presented in some detail elsewhere (Shneidman 1967, 1971, 1973). . . .

Suicide Statistics: Some Questions

In relation to suicide statistics in the United States, we know that accurate figures do not now exist. There is widespread confusion and considerable difference of interpretation as to how to classify deaths. For example, what is considered suicide in one locality is often reported as accidental death in another. The factors that determine decisions of coroners and medical examiners must be made clearly visible as attempts are made to develop criteria for gathering vital baseline data in the area of suicide.

There is an urgent need to explore and describe present practices of reporting suicides and the degree of consistency or inconsistency of such reporting in the United States. Until such information is obtained, it will be impossible to interpret the available statistics. The coroners and medical examiners are the keys to the meaningful reporting of statistics on suicide.

It is believed that it is of the highest priority that an investigation be focused around the following questions directly related to this problem:

1. What percentage of all deaths are autopsied?

2. Who, at present, are the certifying officials, officers, or agencies? Are these medical examiners, physicians in the community, sheriffs, coroners? How are they selected? how trained?

3. What are the present official criteria given to certifying officials in various jurisdictions to guide them in reporting a death as suicide?

4. What are the present actual practices of certifying officials in reporting suicidal deaths? To what extent are these practices consistent with or different from the official criteria?

5. By what actual processes do the certifying officials arrive at the decision to list a death as suicide?

6. How often are autopsies performed? Who determines when an autopsy is to be performed? Are the services of a toxicologist and biochemist available?

7. What percentage of deaths are seen as equivocal, or undetermined, or as a combination of two or more modes (for example, accident-suicide, undetermined)?

8. What are the criteria for special procedures in an equivocal death?

9. How much of the total investigation of a death is dependent upon the police reports? What is the relationship of the coroner's investigation to the local police department?

10. When, if ever, are behavioral or social scientists involved in the total investigatory procedure of a death?

11. What percentage of certifying officials in the United States are medically trained? Does medical training significantly influence the way in which deaths are reported?

From data dealing with these questions, based on appropriate sampling from regions and taking into account rural-urban differences, size of municipalities, etc., appropriate agencies could then address themselves to a number of important general questions, including the following:

- What local, State, regional, or other differences emerge in the practices of reporting the various modes of death?
- What are the general implications from the data for the accuracy of present death statistics, especially the statistics for each separate mode?
- What suggestions can be made for improvement in conceptualization, practice, and training which point toward more accurate and meaningful reporting?

Suggestions for the Conceptual Improvement of the Death Certificate

The current NASH classification of death grew out of a 17th century way of thinking about man (as a biological vessel who was subject to whims of fate) and tended to leave man himself out of his own death. Twentieth century psychology and psychiatry have attempted to put man—conscious and unconscious—back into his own life, including the way in which he dies. The NASH classification of modes of death is not only apsychological but it tends to emphasize relatively unimportant details. For example, it is essentially a matter of indifference to a human being whether a light fixture above him falls and he is invaded by a lethal chandelier (accidental mode), or someone about him coughs and he is invaded by a lethal virus (natural mode), or someone shoots a gun at him and he is invaded by a lethal bullet (homicidal mode), if the fact is that he does not wish (intention) any of these events to occur.

In order to avoid the inadequacies of this conceptual confusion, it has been proposed that all human deaths be classified among three types: intentioned, subintentioned, and unintentioned (Shneidman 1963, 1973).

An *intentioned* death is any death in which the decedent plays a direct, conscious role in effecting his own demise. On the other hand, an *unintentioned* death is any death, whatever its determined cause or apparent NASH mode, in which the decedent plays no effective role in effecting his own demise—where death is due entirely to independent physical trauma from without, or to non-psychologically laden biological failure from within.

But most importantly—and, in a fashion I believe to be characteristic of a sizable percentage of all deaths—*subintentioned* deaths are deaths in which the decedent plays some partial, covert, or unconscious role in hastening his own demise. The objective evidences of the presence of these roles lie in such behavioral manifestations as, for example, poor judgment, excessive risk-taking, abuse of alcohol, misuse of drugs, neglect of self, self-destructive style of life, disregard of prescribed life-saving medical regimen, and so on, where the individual fosters, facilitates, exacerbates, or hastens the process of his dying.

That individuals may play an unconscious role in their own failures and act inimically to their own best welfare and even hasten their own deaths seems to be well documented in the general clinical practice. Included in this subintention category would be many patterns of mismanagement and brink-of-death living which result in death. In terms of the traditional classification of modes of death (natural, accident, homicide, and suicide), some instances of all four types can be subsumed under this category, depending on the particular details of each case.

Confusion also discolors and obfuscates our thinking in the field of suicide. Currently there is much overattention paid to the categories of attempted, threatened, and committed suicide. These categories are confusing because they do not tell us with what intensity the impulse was felt or the deed was done. One can attempt to attempt, attempt to commit, or attempt to feign, and so on. One can threaten or attempt suicide at any level of intensity. What is needed is a dimension which cuts across these labels and permits us to evaluate the individual's drive to self-imposed death. I propose a dimension called *lethality*, defined as the probability of a specific individual's killing himself (i.e., ending up dead) in the immediate future (today, tomorrow, the next day—not next month). A measure of the lethality of any individual can be made at any given time. When we say that individual is "suicidal" we mean to convey the idea that he is experiencing an acute exacerbation (or heightening) of his lethality. All suicide attempts, suicide threats, and committed suicides should be rated for their lethality. The rule of thumb would be that beyond a certain point one must be wary of the danger of explosion into overt behavior.

What is suggested is that, *in addition* to the present NASH classification, each death certificate contain a new supplementary item which reflects the individual's lethality intent. This item might be labeled *Imputed Lethality* (recognizing its inferential character) and would consist of four terms, one of which would then be checked. The terms are: *High, Medium, Low, Absent,* and would be defined as follows.

High lethality. The decedent definitely wanted to die; the decedent played a direct conscious role in his own death; the death was due primarily to the decedent's openly conscious wish or desire to be dead, or to his (her) actions in carrying out that wish (e.g., jumping rather than falling or being pushed from a high place; he shot himself to death; he deliberately interrupted or refused lifesaving procedures or medical regimen).

Medium lethality. The decedent played an important role in effecting or hastening his own death. Death was due in some part to actions of the decedent in which he played some partial, covert, or unconscious role in hastening his own demise. The evidences for this lie in the decedent's behaviors, such as his carelessness, foolhardiness, neglect of self, imprudence, poor judgment, provoking others, disregard of prescribed life-saving medical regimen, active resignation to death, mismanagement of drugs, abuse of alcohol, "tempting fate," "asking for trouble," etc., where the decedent himself seemed to have fostered, facilitated, or hastened the process of his dying, or the date of his death.

Low lethality. The decedent played some small but not insignificant role in effecting or hastening his own demise. The same as medium above, but to a much less degree.

Absent lethality. The decedent played no role in effecting his own death. The death was due entirely to assault from outside the body (in a situation where the decedent played no role in causing this to happen), or death was due entirely to failure within the body (in a decedent who wished to continue to live).

The item on the certificate might look like this:

IMPUTED LETHALITY: (Check One)
High   Medium   Low   Absent
(See Instructions)

The reasons for advocating the suggestion are as follows: First, this classification permits reflection of the role that the dead individual played in his own dying, in hastening his own death; the ways in which he might have participated in his own death, etc. Next, it is more fair. At present, individuals of higher social status who commit suicide are more likely to be assigned the mode of accidental or natural death than are individuals of lower social status who no more evidently commit suicide. If the term is to have any meaning at all, it should be fairly used across the board, measured by the individual's intention. Finally, the lethality intention item provides an unexampled source of information by means of which biostatisticians, public health officials, and social scientists could assess the mental health of any community. It is obvious that the number of deaths that are caused, hoped for, or hastened by the decedents themselves is a measure of the prevalence of psychological disorder and social stress. At present we do not have this measure, and we need it.

It might be protested, inasmuch as the assessments of these intention states involve the appraisal of unconscious factors, that some workers (especially lay coroners) cannot legitimately be expected to make the kinds of psychological judgments required for this type of classification. To this, my answer would be that medical examiners and coroners throughout the country are making judgments of precisely this nature every day of the week. In the situation of evaluating a possible suicide, the coroner often acts (sometimes without realizing it) as psychiatrist and psychologist, and as both judge and jury in a quasijudicial way. This is because certification of death as suicide does, willy-nilly, imply some judgments or reconstruction of the victim's motivation or intention. Making these judgments—perhaps more coroners ought to use the category of Undetermined—is a part of a coroner's function. But it might be far better if these psychological dimensions were explicit, and an attempt, albeit crude, made to use them, than to have these psychological dimensions employed in an implicit and unverbalized (yet operating) manner. The dilemma is between the polarities of the presently used oversimplified classification, on the one hand, and a somewhat more complex, but more meaningful classification, on the other. The goal should be to try to combine greatest usefulness with maximum meaningfulness.

In Marin County, California, the coroner's office is currently assessing each death processed by that office in terms of *both* the traditional NASH classification of mode of death *and* the lethality intention of the decedent. For a 2-year period, 1971-1972 (978 cases), the breakdown was as follows:*

---

*I am especially grateful to Keith C. Craig, coroner's deputy, Marin County, for his interest and help in supplying these data.

Natural deaths (630): high lethality intent, none; medium lethality, 33 (5%); low, 37 (6%); absent, 560 (89%).
Accidental deaths (176): high lethality intent, 2 (1%); medium, 77 (44%); low, 40 (22%); absent, 57 (33%).
Suicidal deaths (131): high lethality intent, 131 (100%).
Homicidal deaths (37): high lethality intent, none; medium, 20 (54%); low, 9 (24%); absent, 8 (22%).
Four deaths were of unknown origin.

The first thing we notice is that *some* natural, accidental, and homicidal deaths were classified as having *some* degree of lethal intention. If the medium-intention and low-intention categories are combined, then over one-fourth (26%) of all natural, accidental, and homicidal deaths (216 in 843) were deemed to be *subintentioned.* If one then adds the suicidal deaths, in which the decedent has obviously played a role in his own death, then only 64 percent of all deaths (625 in 978) were deemed to have been totally adventitious; conversely, 36 percent were deemed to have had some psychological components.

Also of special interest in these Marin County data is the finding that coroners can, with apparently no more difficulty than they experience in assigning deaths to the NASH categories, simultaneously (and by essentially the same process of inference and induction) assign deaths to intentional categories as well. It is an important pioneer effort and deserves widespread emulation.

In summary, the following points may be emphasized.

Causes. The classification of causes of death has been rather well worked out and is consistent with contemporary knowledge. There is currently an accepted international classification which has world-wide acceptance.

Modes. The modes of death have not been stated explicitly and have not been too well understood. In general, four currently implied modes of death—natural, accidental, suicidal, and homicidal—suffer from the important deficiency of viewing man as a vessel of the fates and omitting entirely his role in his own demise.

Intent. The addition of the dimension of lethal intention serves to modernize the death certificate, just as in the past advances have been made from the teachings of bacteriology, surgery, anesthesiology, immunology, etc.

The time is now long overdue for the meaningful introduction of the psychodynamics of death into the death certificate. The addition of a single item on imputed lethal intent (High, Medium,

Low, Absent) would provide an appropriate reflection of the psychological state of the subject and begin, at last, to reflect the teachings of 20th century psychology. In this way we might again permit the certification of death to reflect accurately our best current understanding of man.

References

Colby, Marian. 1965. The significance, evolution, and implementation of standard certificates. *Am. J. Public Health.* 55:596-99.

Curphey, Theodore J. 1961. The role of the social scientist in the medicolegal certification of death from suicide. *In* Norman L. Faberow and Edwin S. Shneidman, eds., *The Cry for Help.* New York: McGraw-Hill.

Curphey, Theodore J. 1967. The forensic pathologist and the multidisciplinary approach to death. *In* Edwin S. Shneidman, ed., *Essays in Self-Destruction.* New York: Science House.

Hotchner, A.E. 1966. *Papa Hemingway: A Personal Memoir.* New York: Random House.

Litman, Robert E. 1967. Sigmund Freud on suicide. *In* Edwin S. Shneidman, ed., *Essays in Self-Destruction.* New York: Science House.

Litman, Robert E., T.J. Curphey, E.S. Shneidman, N.L. Faberow, and N.D. Tabachnick. 1963. Investigations of equivocal suicides. *J.A.M.A.* 184:924-29.

McGee, Richard K. 1974. *Crisis Intervention in the Community.* Baltimore: University Park Press.

Menninger, Karl A. 1938. *Man Against Himself.* New York: Harcourt, Brace.

Rogow, Arnold A. 1963. *James Forrestal: A Study of Personality, Politics and Policy.* Los Angeles: Boulevard Bookshop.

Shneidman, Edwin S. 1963. Orientations toward death: A vital aspect of the study of lives. *In* Robert W. White, ed., *The Study of Lives.* New York: Atherton.

Shneidman, Edwin S. 1967. Sleep and self-destruction: A phenomenological study. *In* Edwin S. Shneidman, ed., *Essays in Self-Destruction.* New York: Science House.

Shneidman, Edwin S. 1968. Orientations toward cessation: A re-examination of current modes of death. *J. Forensic Sci.* 13:33-45.

Shneidman, Edwin S. 1969. Suicide, lethality, and the psychological autopsy. *In* Edwin S. Shneidman and Magno Ortega, eds., *Aspects of Depression.* Boston: Little, Brown.

Shneidman, Edwin S. 1971. Prevention, intervention, and postvention of suicide. *Ann. Intern. Med.* 75:453-58.

Shneidman, Edwin S. 1973, 1974. *Deaths of Man.* New York: Quadrangle Books; Penguin Books.

Shneidman, Edwin S., and Norman L. Farberow. 1961. Sample investigations of equivocal deaths. *In The Cry for Help.* New York: McGraw-Hill.

Weisman, Avery D. 1974. *The Realization of Death: A Guide for the Psychological Autopsy.* New York: Behavioral Publications.

Weisman, Avery D., and Robert Kastenbaum. 1968. The psychological autopsy. *Community Ment. Health J.* Monograph No. 4. New York: Behavioral Publications.

Wertenbaker, Lael Tucker. 1957. *Death of a Man.* New York: Random House.

World Health Organization. 1957. *Manual of the International Statistical Classification of Diseases, Injuries, and Causes of Death,* Based on the Recommendations of the Seventh Revision Conference, 1955. Geneva: World Health Organization.

Psychotherapy with Suicidal Patients

I t seems logical that before we consider what the psychotherapy of a suicidal person ought to be that we have some common understanding of the suicidal state itself. Of course, everybody agrees that suicide is an enormously complicated term, encompassing a wide variety (and different ranges) of dysphoria, disturbance, self-abnegation, resignation, terror-cum-pain—to mention but a few inner states that are involved. . . .

Suicide is the human act of self-inflicted, self-intended cessation (i.e., the permanent stopping of consciousness). It is best understood as a bio-socio-psychologico-existential state of malaise. It is obviously not a disease and just as obviously a number of kinds of trained individuals other than physicians can help individuals who are in a suicidal state.

If we are to escape many of the current somewhat simplistic notions of suicide (especially those which totally equate a disease called suicide with a disease called depression), then we need to explicate what the suicidal state of mind is like. Our key source in this can be the ordinary dictionary—eschewing any nomenclature of technical and, especially, technically diagnostic terms. In the dictionary there are words, e.g., angered, anguished, cornered. dependent, frustrated, guilty, helpless, hopeless, hostile, rageful, shamed, that will help us in our understanding. For us, in this chapter, two less common (but ordinary) dictionary words— *perturbation* and *lethality*—will be the keystone words of our understanding.

Perturbation refers to how upset (disturbed, agitated, sane-insane, discomposed) the individual is—rated, let's say, on a 1 to 9 scale. Lethality refers to how lethal the individual is, i.e., how likely it is that he will take his own life—also rated on a 1 to 9 scale.

From *Specialized Techniques in Individual Psychotherapy* (edited by T.B. Karasu and L. Bellak), 1980, pp. 305-313. Reprinted with permission of Brunner/Mazel.

At the outset, I need to indicate what kinds of suicidal states I am talking about in order to indicate what kinds of psychotherapy are appropriate for them. We can arbitrarily divide the seriousness (or risk, or lethality, or suicidality) of all suicidal efforts (actions, deeds, events, episodes)—whether verbalizations (ordinarily called threats) or behaviors (ordinarily called attempts)—into three rough commonsense groupings: low, medium and high. In this chapter, I shall focus on the suicidal events or deeds of *high* lethality, where the danger of self-inflicted death is realistically large and imminent; what one might ordinarily call high suicide risks. Of course, a suicide act (deed, occurrence, event, threat, attempt) *of whatever lethality* is always a genuine psychiatric situation and should be treated without any iatrogenic elements. Thus, in the treatment of the suicidal person there is almost never any place for the therapist's hostility, anger, sardonic attitudes, daring the patient, or pseudo-democratic indifference.

By focusing solely on the *psychotherapeutic* approaches to high suicide risks, it should be obvious at the beginning that this chapter is a moiety—omitting entirely (and advertently) the lively areas of treatment suicidal individuals receive by means of chemical, electrical or institutional modalities.

Theoretically, the treatment of an acutely highly suicidal person is quite simple: It consists, almost by definition, of lowering his lethality level; in practice, this is usually done by decreasing or mollifying his level of perturbation. In short, we defuse the situation (like getting the gun), we create activity of support and care around the person, and we make that person's temporarily unbearable life just enough better so that he or she can stop to think and reconsider. *The way to decrease lethality is by dramatically decreasing the felt perturbation.*

Working intensively with a highly suicidal person—someone who might be assessed as 7, 8 or 9 on a 1 to 9 scale of lethality—as distinguished from someone of moderate or low lethality, is different from almost any other human encounter, with the possible exception of that of working intensively with a dying person—but that is another story. Psychotherapy with an intensely suicidal person is a special task; it demands a different kind of involvement. The goal is different—not that of increasing comfort, which is the goal of most ordinary psychotherapy, but the more primitive goal of simply keeping the person alive. The rules are therefore different, and it follows (or rather precedes) that the theoretical rationale is different.

A t this juncture, I wish to make a distinction among *four* psychologically different kinds of human encounters: conversation (or "ordinary talk"); an hierarchical exchange; psychotherapy or a "professional exchange"; and, finally, clinical suicidology or working psychologically with a highly lethal person.

In ordinary talk or conversation, the focus is on the surface content (concrete events, specific dates, ordinary details); on what is actually being said; on the obviously stated meanings; on the ordinary interesting (or uninteresting) details of life. Further, the social role between the two speakers is one in which the two participants are essentially equal. Each participant has the social right to ask the other the same questions which he or she has been asked by the other. The best example of ordinary talk is two friends conversing with one another.

In a hierarchical verbal exchange the two participants are socially, and hence psychologically, unequal. This difference may be imposed by the situation, such as the exchange between a military officer and an enlisted person, or it may be agreed to by the two involved parties, such as between a physician and a patient. In either instance, the two are not psychologically equal. For example, an officer or a physician can ask an enlisted person or a patient, respectively, certain personal questions to which a rational response is expected, that the person of "lower status" could not ask the other person in return without appearing impertinent or aberrant. Yet most of the talk is still on the surface, concerning the real details of everyday life.

In a professional psychotherapeutic exchange the focus is on feelings, emotional content and unconscious meanings, rather than on what is apparently being said. The emphasis is on the latent (between-the-lines) significance of what is being said more than on the manifest and obvious content; on the unconscious meanings, including double-entendres, puns, and slips-of-the-tongue; on themes that run as common threads through the content, rather than on the concrete details for their own sake. Perhaps the most distinguishing aspect of the professional exchange (as opposed to ordinary talk) is the occurrence of transference, wherein the patient projects onto the therapist certain deep expectations and feelings. These transference reactions often stem from the patient's childhood and reflect neurotic patterns of reaction (of love, hate, dependency, suspicion, etc.) to whatever the therapist may or may not be doing. The therapist is often invested by the patient with almost magical healing powers, which, in fact, can serve as a self-fulfilling prophecy and thus help the interaction become therapeutic for the patient. In this paragraph, the use of the words therapist and patient already implies that, of the two parties, one has tacitly agreed to seek assistance and the other has agreed to try to give it. The roles of the two participants, unlike those in a conversation, are, in this respect, not co-equal. A therapist and a patient could not simply exchange roles.

In working as a clinical suicidologist with an individual who is highly suicidal, the focus is again different. In this situation, the attention is primarily on the lethality. Most importantly, what differentiates this modality of therapy from any other psychotherapy is the handling of the transference feelings. Specifically, the transference (from the patient to the therapist) and the counter-transference (from the therapist to the patient)—especially those positive feelings of affection and concern—can legitimately be much more intense and more deep than would be seemly or appropriate (or even ethical) in ordinary psychotherapy where time is assumed to be endless and where it is taken for granted that the patient will continue functioning in life.

Working with a highly suicidal person demands a different kind of involvement. There may be as important a conceptual difference between ordinary psychotherapy (with individuals where dying or living is not *the* issue) and psychotherapy with acutely suicidal persons as there is between ordinary psychotherapy and ordinary talk.

The main point of working with a lethally-oriented person—in the give-and-take of talk, the advice, the interpretations, the listening—is to increase that individual's psychological sense of possible choices and sense of being emotionally supported. Relatives, friends and colleagues should, after they are assessed to be on the life-side of the individual's ambivalence, be closely involved in the total treatment process. Suicide prevention is not best done as a solo practice. A combination of consultation, ancillary therapists and the use of all the interpersonal and community resources that one can involve is, in general, the best way of proceeding.

Recall that we are talking about psychotherapy with the highly suicidal persons—not one of low or even medium lethality. With this in mind—and keeping in mind also the four psychological components of the suicidal state of mind (heightened inimicality, elevated perturbation, conspicuous constriction of intellectual focus, and the idea of cessation as a solution)—then relatively simple formula for treatment can be stated. That formulation concentrates on two of the four psychological components, specifically on the constriction and the perturbation. Simply put, the way to save a highly suicidal person is to decrease the constriction, that is, to widen the range of possible thoughts and fantasies (*from* the dichotomous two—either one specific outcome or death—*to* at least three or more possibilities for admittedly less-than-perfect solution), and, most importantly—without which the attempt to broaden the constriction will not work—to decrease the individual's perturbation.

How does a psychotherapist decrease the elevated perturbation of a highly suicidal person? Answer: by doing anything and almost everthing possible to cater to the infantile idiosyncrasies, the dependency needs, the sense of pressure and futility, the feelings of hopelessness and helplessness that the individual is experiencing. In order to help a highly lethal person, one should involve others; create activity around the person; do what he or she wants done—and, if that cannot be accomplished, at least move in the direction of the desired goals to some substitute goals that approximate those which have been lost. Remember that life—and remind the patient of this fact (in a kindly but oracular way)—is often the choice among lousy alternatives. The key to functioning, to wisdom and to life itself is often to choose the least lousy alternative that is practicably attainable.

Taken down to its bare roots, the principle is: To decrease lethality one puts a hook on perturbation and, doing what needs to be done, pulls the level of perturbation down—and with that action brings down the active level of lethality. Then, when the person is no longer highly suicidal—then the usual methods of psychotherapy (which are not the subject for this chapter) can be usefully employed.

As to how to help a suicidal individual, it is best to look upon any suicidal act, whatever its lethality, as an effort by an individual to stop unbearable anguish or intolerable pain by "doing something." Knowing this usually guides us as to what the treatment should be. In the same sense, the way to save a person's life is also to "do something." Those "somethings" include putting that information (that the person is in trouble with himself) into the stream of communication, letting others know about it, breaking what could be a fatal secret, talking to the person, talking to others, proferring help, getting loved ones interested and responsive, creating action around the person, showing response, indicating interest, and, if possible, showing deep concern.

I conclude with an example—actually a composite of several actual highly suicidal persons I have known.

Case Study

A young woman in her 20s, a nurse at the hospital where I worked, asked me pleadingly if I would see her teenage sister whom she believed to be highly suicidal. The attractive, younger woman—agitated and tearful but coherent—told me (in the privacy of my office) that she was single, pregnant and determined to kill herself. She showed me a small automatic pistol she had in her purse. Her being pregnant was such a mortal shame to her, combined with strong feelings of rage and guilt, that she simply could not "bear to live" (or live to bear?). Suicide was the *only* alternative, and shooting herself was the *only* way to do it. Either she had to be unpregnant (the way she was before she conceived) or she had to be dead.

I did several things. For one, I took out a sheet of paper and—to begin to "widen her blinders"—said something like, "Now, let's see: You could have an abortion here locally." ("I couldn't do that.") It is precisely the "can'ts" and the "won'ts" and "have to's" and "nevers" and "always" and "onlys" that are to be negotiated in psychotherapy. "You could go away and have an abortion." ("I couldn't do that.") "You could bring the baby to term and keep the baby." ("I couldn't do that.") "You could have the baby and adopt it out." ("I couldn't do that.") "We could get in touch with the young man involved." ("I couldn't do that.") "We could involve the help of your parents." ("I couldn't do that.") and "You can always commit suicide, but there is obviously no need to do that today." (No response.) "Now first, let me take that gun, and then let's look at this *list* and rank them in order and see what their advantages, disadvantages and implications are, remembering that none of them may be perfect."

The very making of this list, my professional and nonhortatory and nonjudgmental approach already had a calming influence on her. Within 15 minutes her lethality had begun to deescalate. She actually rank-ordered the list, commenting negatively on each item, but what was of critical importance was that suicide, which I included in the total realistic list, was now ranked third—no longer first or second.

She decided that she would, reluctantly, want to talk to the father of her child. Not only had they never discussed the "issue," but he did not even know about it. But there was a formidable obstacle: He lived in another city, almost across the country and that involved (what seemed to be a big item in the patient's mind) a long distance call. It was a matter of literally seconds to ascertain the area code from the long distance operator, to obtain his telephone number from information, and then—obviously with some trepidation and keen ambivalence for her—to dial his number (at university expense), with the support of my presence to speak to him directly.

The point is not how the issue was practically resolved, without an excessive number of deep or shallow interpretations as to why she permitted herself to become pregnant and other aspects of her relationships with men, etc. What is important is that it was possible to achieve the assignment of that day: to lower her lethality.

In general, any suicidal state is characterized by its transient quality, its pervasive ambivalence, and its dyadic nature. Psychiatrists and other health professionals are well advised to minimize, if not totally to disregard, those probably well-intentioned but shrill writings in this field which naively speak of an individual's "right to commit suicide"—a right which, in actuality, cannot be denied—as though the suicidal person were a chronic univalently self-destructive hermit.

A number of special features in the management of a highly lethal patient can be mentioned. Some of these special therapeutic stratagems or orientations with a highly lethal patient attend to or reflect the *transient, ambivalent* and *dyadic* aspects of almost all suicidal acts.

1. A continuous, preferably daily, monitoring of the patient's lethality rating.
2. An active out-reach; being willing to deal with some of the reality problems of the patient openly, where advisable; giving direction (sans exhortation) to the patient; actively taking the side of life. It relates to befriending and caring.
3. Use of community resources including employment, Veterans Administration (when applicable), social agencies, and psychiatric social work assistance.
4. Consultation. There is almost no instance in a therapist's professional life when consultation with a peer is as important as when he is dealing with a highly suicidal patient. The items to be discussed might include the therapist's treatment of the case; his own feelings of frustration, helplessness or even anger; his countertransference reactions generally; the advisability of hospitalization for the patient, etc.
5. Hospitalization. Hospitalization is always a complicating event in the treatment of a suicidal patient but it should not, on those grounds, be eschewed. Obviously, the quality of care—from doctors, nurses and attendants—is crucial. Stoller, discussing one of his complex long-range cases, says: "... there were several other factors without which the therapy might not have succeeded. First, the hospital. The patient's life could not have been saved if a hospital had not been immediately available *and a few of the personnel familiar with me and the patient.*"*
6. Transference. As in almost no other situation and at almost no other time, the successful treatment of a highly suicidal person depends

---

*Robert J. Stoller. *Splitting*. New York: Quadrangle Books, 1973.

heavily on the transference. The therapist can be active, show his personal concern, increase the frequency of the sessions, invoke the "magic" of the unique therapist-patient relationship, be less of a *tabula rasa*, give "transfusions" of (realistic) hope and succorance. In a figurative sense, I believe that Eros can work wonders against Thanatos.

7. The involvement of significant others. Suicide is most often a highly charged dyadic crisis. It follows from this that the therapist, unlike his usual practice of dealing almost exclusively with his patient (and even fending off the spouse, the lover, parents, grown children), should consider the advisability of working directly with the significant others. For example, if the individual is married, it is important to meet the spouse. The therapist must assess whether, in fact, the spouse is suicidogenic; whether they ought to be separated; whether there are misunderstandings which the therapist can help resolve; or whether the spouse is insightful and concerned and can be used by the therapist as an ally and co-therapist. The same is true for homosexual lovers, for patient and parent, etc. It is not suggested that the significant other be seen as often as the patient is seen, but that other real people in the suicidal patient's life be directly involved and, at the minimum, their role as hinderer or helper in the treatment process be assessed.

8. Careful modification of the usual canons of confidentiality. Admittedly, this is a touchy and complicated point, but the therapist should not ally himself with death. Statements given during the therapy session relating to the patient's overt suicidal (or homicidal) plans obviously cannot be treated as a "secret" between two collusive partners. In the previous example of the patient who opened her purse and showed me a small automatic pistol with which she said she was going, that day, to kill herself, two obvious interpretations would be that she obviously wanted me to take the weapon from her, or that she was threatening me. In any event, I told her that she could not leave my office with the gun and insisted that she hand her purse to me. She countered by saying that I had abrogated the basic rule of therapy, namely that she could tell me anything. I pointed out that "anything" did not mean committing suicide and that she must know that I could not be a partner in that kind of enterprise. For a moment she seemed angered and then relieved; she gave me the gun. The rule is to "defuse" the potentially lethal situation. To have left her with a loaded gun would also leave her with a latent message.

9. Limitation of one's own practice to a very few highly lethal patients. It is possible to see a fairly large number of moderate and low-rated lethal patients in one's patient load, but one or two *highly* lethal patients seem to be the superhuman limit for most therapists at any given time. Such patients demand a great deal of investment of psychic energy and one must beware of spreading oneself too thin in his or her own professional life.

Working with highly suicidal persons borrows from the goals of crisis intervention: not to take on and ameliorate the individual's entire personality structure and to cure all the neuroses, but simply to keep him or her alive. That is the *sine qua non* without which no human being can function—and no therapy would have meaning.

Postvention:
The Care of the Bereaved

G rief and mourning are not diseases, but their deleterious and inimical effects can often be as serious as though they were. The recently bereaved person is typically bereft and disorganized. Long-standing habit patterns of intimate interpersonal responses are irreversibly severed. There is a concomitant gale of strong feelings, usually including abandonment and despair, sometimes touching upon guilt and anger, and almost always involving a sense of crushing emptiness and loss. In light of these psychological realities it comes as no surprise that individuals who are acutely bereaved constitute a population "at risk."

Excluding Freud's indispensible paper, "Mourning and Melancholia," published in 1917, much of the important work on this topic has been done only since 1944. In general, these studies point out that grief and mourning may have serious physical and psychological concomitants (in the way of heightened morbidity and even a greater risk of death), and they explicate some of the dimensions of bereavement as well as ways of helping the bereaved.

This chapter will not be an attempt to replow the ground so fertilely turned by others, especially Parkes in his chapter "Helping the Bereaved" in his book *Bereavement* in which he discusses the role of the funeral director, the church, the family doctor, and self-help organizations, among others. Instead, the discussion will be limited to what I know best, namely, my own work with bereaved persons. . . .

Purpose of Postvention

I prefer to think of the work with the bereaved person as a process that I have called *postvention*: those appropriate and helpful acts that come *after* the dire event itself. The reader will recognize prevention, intervention, and postvention as roughly synonymous with the traditional health con-

From *Consultation-Liaison Psychiatry* (edited by Robert O. Pasnau), 1975, pp. 245-256. Reprinted with permission of Grune and Stratton.

cepts of primary, secondary, and tertiary prevention, or with the concepts of immunization, treatment, and rehabilitation. Lindemann has referred to "preventive intervention." It would be simpler to speak of postvention.

As I have described in *Deaths of Man*, postvention consists of those activities that serve to reduce the aftereffects of a traumatic event in the lives of the survivors. Its purpose is to help survivors live longer, more productively, and less stressfully than they are likely to do otherwise. I will attempt to summarize my observations in the following paragraphs.

Reactions of Survivor Victims

It is obvious that some deaths are more stigmatizing or traumatic than others: death by murder, or by the neglect of oneself or some other person, or by suicide. Survivor victims of such deaths are invaded by an unhealthy complex of disturbing emotions: shame, guilt, hatred, perplexity. They are obsessed with thoughts about the death, seeking reasons, casting blame, and often punishing themselves.

The investigations of widows by Parkes are most illuminating. The principal finding of his studies is that independent of her age, a woman who has lost a husband recently is more likely to die (from alcoholism, malnutrition, or a variety of disorders related to neglect of self, disregard of a prescribed medical regimen or common-sense precautions, or even a seemingly unconscious boredom with life), or to be physically ill, or emotionally disturbed than nonwidowed women. The findings seem to imply that grief is itself a dire process, almost akin to a disease, and that there are subtle factors at work that can take a heavy toll unless they are treated and controlled.

These striking results had been intuitively known long before they were empirically demonstrated. The efforts of Lindemann, Caplan, and Silverman to aid survivors of "heavy deaths" were postventions based on the premise of heightened risk in bereaved persons. Lindemann's work, which led to his formulations of acute grief and crisis intervention, began with his treatment of the survivors of the tragic Coconut Grove nightclub fire in Boston in 1942 in which 499 people died. Silverman's projects, under the direction of Caplan, have centered around a widow-to-widow program. These efforts bear obvious similarities with the programs of "befriending" practiced by the Samaritans, an organization founded by Reverend Chad Varah in 1966 and most active in Great Britain.

Death a "Disaster"

A case can be made for viewing the sudden death of a loved one as a *disaster* and, using the verbal bridge provided by that concept, learning from the professional literature on conventionally recognized disasters—those sudden, unexpected events, such as earthquakes and large-scale explosions, that cause a large number of deaths and have widespread effects. Wolfenstein has described a "disaster syndrome": a "combination of emotional dullness, unresponsiveness to outer stimulation and inhibition of activity. The individual who has just undergone disaster is apt to suffer from at least a transitory sense of worthlessness; his usual capacity for self-love becomes impaired."

A similar psychological contraction is seen in the initial shock reaction to catastrophic news—death, failure, disclosure, disgrace, the keenest personal loss. Studies of a disastrous ship sinking by Friedman and Lum and of the effects of a tornado by Wallace both describe an initial psychic shock followed by motor retardation, flattening of affect, somnolence, amnesia, and suggestibility. There is marked increase in dependency needs with regressive behavior and traumatic loss of feelings of identity and, overall, a kind of "affective anesthesia." There is an unhealthy docility, a cowed and subdued reaction. One is reminded of Lifton's description of "psychic closing off" and "psychic numbing" among the Hibakusha, the survivors of the atomic bomb dropped on Hiroshima:

> Very quickly—sometimes within minutes or even seconds—Hibakusha began to undergo a process of "psychic closing off"; that is, they simply ceased to feel. They had a clear sense of what was happening around them, but their emotional reactions were unconsciously turned off. Others' immersion in larger responsibilities was accompanied by a greater form of closing off which might be termed "psychic numbing."

Postvention: An Ongoing Therapy

Postventive efforts are not limited to this initial stage of shock; they are more often directed to the longer haul, the day-to-day living with grief over a year or more following the first shock of loss. Typically postvention extends over months during that critical first year, and it shares many of the characteristics of psychotherapy: talk, abreaction, interpretation, reassurance, direction, and even gentle confrontation. It provides an arena for the expression of guarded emotions, especially such negative affective states as anger, shame, and guilt. It puts a measure of stability into the grieving person's life and provides an interpersonal relationship with the therapist that can be genuine, in that honest feelings need not be suppressed or dissembled.

Parkes distinguishes four phases in the bereavement process: numbness, yearning/protest, disorganization, and reorganization—but in general we ought to view "stages" of recovery from death (and especially we need to view the so-called stages of the dying process) with a liberal and flexible mind.

Characteristics of the Postventive Session

In order to appreciate the nature of postvention, it is necessary to touch upon some important characteristics of the interaction between the bereaved victim and the therapist,* specifically the difference between a *conversation* (or "ordinary talk") and a *professional exchange*—recognizing that postventive efforts should be of the latter sort. This distinction is exceptionally elementary, but because this understanding is at the very heart of effective postventive work, these rudimentary ideas need to be made explicit. The differences between the two can be charted in the form of some contrasts between ordinary talk (e.g., "I'm so sorry to hear about the death." "Please accept my most sincere condolescences." "Time will heal the wounds.") and a professional exchange.

Conversation	*Professional Exchange*
Content	
Substantive content, i.e., the talk is primarily about things, events, dates—the surface of the world.	Affective (emotional) content, i.e., the exchange focuses (not constantly but occasionally) on the feelings and the emotional tone of the patient, sometimes minimizing the "facts."

---

*The person who systematically attempts to help the bereaved individual is either a therapist or is acting in the role of a therapist. He cannot escape this role. This is not to say that many others—relatives, dear friends, organization (e.g., church) members, neighbors—do not play important, perhaps the most important, roles.

Level

Manifest level, i.e., conversation focuses on what is said, the actual words that are uttered, the facts that are stated.

Latent level, i.e., the professional person listens for what is "between the lines," below the surface, what is implied, not expressed or only unconsciously present.

Meanings

Conscious meanings, i.e., in ordinary speech we deal with the other person as though what was said was meant and as though the person were "a rational man" and that he "knows his own mind."

Unconscious meanings, i.e., there is a whole flow of the mind that is not immediately available at any given moment to the person and that there are unconscious meanings and latent intentions in human exchanges. We listen for hidden meanings and latent implications.

Abstraction

Phenotypic abstraction, i.e., there is concern with the ordinary interesting details of life, where no set of details necessarily bears any relationship to any other set.

Genotypic abstraction, i.e., the therapist is always looking for congruencies, similarities, commonalities, *generalizations* about the patient's psychological life. These constitute the understanding by the therapist (and are the reservoir of his possible interpretations to the patient).

Role

Social role, i.e., in a conversation or ordinary discourse people are coequals (like neighbors or friends) or depend on the prestige of age, rank, status, and so on, but essentially the relationship is

Transference, i.e., a professional exhange is not talk between two coequals. Rather it is a very special kind of exchange between one person who wishes help (and tacitly agrees to play the patient's role) and another between two people who have equal right to display themselves.

person who agrees to proffer help (and thus is cast in the role of physician, priest, father, magician, witch doctor, helper). Much of what is effective in the exchange is the patient's "transference" onto the therapist. Some of the effectiveness of the therapeutic exchange lies in the power of the "self-fulfilling prophecy."

An example may be useful. Late one afternoon a beautiful 19-year-old girl was stabbed to death by an apparent would-be rapist in a government building. Within an hour her parents were shattered by the news given to them by two rather young, well-meaning but inexperienced policemen. The victim was the couple's only child. Their immediate reactions were shock, disbelief, overwhelming grief, and mounting rage, most of it directed at the agency where the murder had occured.

A few days later, right after the funeral, they were in the office of a high official who was attempting to tender his condolences when the mother said in an anguished tone: "There is nothing you can do!" To which, with good persence of mind, he answered that while it was true that the girl could not be brought back to life, there was something that could be done. Whether he knew the term or not, it was postvention that he had in mind. He brought them, personally, to my office.

I began seeing the parents, usually together, sometimes separately. The principal psychological feature was the mother's anger. I permitted her to voice her grief and to vent her rage (sometimes at me), while I retained the role of the voice of reason: empathizing with the parents' state, recognizing the legitimacy of their feelings when I could but not agreeing when in good conscience I could not agree. I felt that I was truly their friend, and I believed that they felt so too. I had insisted that each of them see a physician for a physical examination. A few months after the brutal murder, the mother developed serious symptoms that required major surgery, from which she made a good recovery. The situation raises the intriguing (and unanswerable) question in my mind whether or not that organic flurry would have occurred if she had not suffered the shock of her daughter's death. In the year following her daughter's death the mother had two extended hospitalizations. Several months after the tragedy the parents seemed to be in rather good shape, physically and emotionally, everything considered. They still had low-level grief and no doubt always will. Here is an edited verbatim portion of a session exactly one year after the death.

DR. S: Is today a year?

MRS. A: Exactly one year. And just about this time when she was killed . . .

DR. S: Where are you both today? Can you sketch the course of your grief?

MRS. A: Well, at first it was extremely intense. It was actually a physical pain. For a couple of months I went around and it hurt—it actually hurt in here. And I felt like I was carrying the world on my shoulders and inside of me.

MR. A: I don't think the pain was physical, it was . . .

MRS. A: No, it wasn't. I mean I felt it physically, but it was a mental pain too.

MR. A: There are times when the pain is still there. It's hard to describe it, it's just there, feeling of pain. I guess it's part of sorrow. We had a very bad day yesterday, much more so than today.

MRS. A: You can't just cut off 19 years in one day. It was like losing an arm or a leg or a head or something. Or a head, because you can do without an arm, and you learn to do in a way, without a daughter. It sounds trite when you say it that way.

MR. A: I think one of the things that has happened in the past year is that, so far as I'm concerned, I don't think I've discussed it too much, but I'm more capable of facing the situation, of thinking about it. I used to try to put it out of my mind. For a while there, the hardest thing I had to do was look at her picture.

DR. S: Do you still have that in your house, do you have it displayed?

MRS. A: Yeah.

MR. A: We have one in our bedroom on the bureau. It stays there all the time, but, uh, I don't get a shock anymore when I look at her picture.

MRS. A: I still turn around when I see blond hair bobbing up and down and I still turn to look, and then I realize how stupid it is. She couldn't look like that anymore. A little girl lives down the street, that I sometimes see, and she walks like she walked. And it still plays tricks, I still look to see if it's her. And sometimes the other children say or do something and it's always in the back of our minds, always in the back of my mind anyway. I think these meetings with you have been very good for us, because there was someone we could talk to. And someone that could show—in a way—take a different viewpoint. How can we see beyond our noses when we're so grief stricken and, oh, I don't know.

MR. A: That's what I was trying to bring out a while ago, that is that you've helped us, me in facing the truth.

DR. S: How was that done?

MR. A: I don't know; just the fact that I was discussing rather freely and maybe . . .

Mrs. A: And we thought we could tell you anything and you wouldn't be angry or, I don't know exactly how to say it, but I always felt we could talk to you and we could tell you exactly what we thought and not face any recriminations or anything like that.

Dr. S: Speaking of anger and recriminations, there was a time—isn't this so—that you were just terribly angry?

Mrs. A: Yes.

Dr. S: What has happened to that anger?

Mrs. A: It's dissipated. At first, in the beginning, I was ready to kill everybody and anybody.

Dr. S: Including me.

Mrs. A: Including you because you represented the government to us.

Mr. A: No, really?

Mrs. A: Yes, in a way he did because I blamed the government for her death. I still feel that somebody here helped. Somebody here helped, and he must know. Whoever it is; who helped, did his part in getting her killed. By not patroling the building, by not doing—a sin of omission is just as big as a big sin of comission. I mean they knew darn well that the building was not safe.

Dr. S: So there are still certainly reservoirs of anger and blame.

Mrs. A: At the time I wanted the murderer caught and killed. Now I would just like him stopped, but I don't want him killed. Will that bring her back? But people were afraid of us. They were afraid to talk to us.

Mr. A: Some still are.

Mrs. A: Some of them still are because they didn't know what to say. It was a difficult thing; it's a difficult thing for most people to find words of sympathy. What do you tell parents whose daughter is killed like that? Another thing that in a way you taught me is to take one day at a time.

Dr. S: How did I teach you that?

Mrs. A: I don't know how, but that's what I've been doing, taking one day at a time. You were able really to show us in a proper perspective. That's one of the things you did; you were always the one to look at things in a straight manner. How could we when we were so prejudiced about anything—I mean about what happened to her. We are so close to the forest, we can't see the trees.

Mr. A: I think you've also managed to curtail her anger in general to a certain extent. Because she was mad at the whole world at the time—any reason. She'd get mad, get ready to prosecute her soup.

Dr. S: Have there been some changes in your general character?

Mrs. A: I think so, I've probably been a little bit more tolerant.

Dr. S: What do you think will happen now in the next year or two?

Mrs. A: We get more used to it. I suppose. He will become more resigned to it; that she isn't here, she won't come back, and that going to the cemetery won't hurt so much. But I try not to make this a special day because what's to celebrate? But it is in a way a special day.

Dr. S: It is an occasion to memorialize.

Mrs. A: It was sad to come home last night and find my husband was crying.

Mr. A: It was just a defense mechanism. I was crying to keep you from crying, so you would feel sorry for me for a change.

MRS. A: I suppose in a way it made me less intolerant of other people. But what a price to have to pay. What a pity. All those years. There is something so final now. I used to feel that there was continuity, that she would have children and in a way live on. My husband is the last of his line. The last male of his line. The last one of his family.

MR. A: It's the end of the name anyway.

DR. S: There is a sense of being cut off from the future, isn't there?

MR. A: I imagine there is going to be a lot of hurt when we have to attend weddings or births.

MRS. A: Somehow it is very hard to think that when you die, that's the end. But it's not as bad as I used to be afraid of death. I am no longer afraid of death personally. It's no longer such a terrible thing. It was terrible, I suppose, because it was unknown. Another time I would have been afraid when I went into the hospital. I was so unafraid that I believed the doctor when he told me before the operation that it wasn't going to hurt. How naive can you be? I wanted to believe it. I don't think, I mean, I'm sure, I could have gone through this past year without my husband.

DR. S: I think you have helped each other in a marvelous way.

MRS. A: I'm really sure that I could never have come through it.

MR. A: Except for one time when she almost walked out on me.

MRS. A: That's different. That didn't count. To get through the impossible days and even longer nights. We weren't perfect, and she was not perfect. Of course, no one will ever bring up any of her faults now.

DR. S: That's so. One doesn't speak ill of the dead.

MRS. A: No. Everybody, when they do talk about her, glosses over any of her faults. No one wants to talk about them. I don't know of anyone who has voluntarily brought up her name but you. Why is there such a taboo? It's been a whole year.

DR. S: Do you feel more than a year older?

MR. A: Very much. We were discussing this not too long ago, and we both felt we had missed out on middle age, that we went from youth to old people.

DR. S: Really. You feel that way?

MRS. A: Most of the time I feel so old and I caught myself talking to my brother and I said when we were young, and he said, "Hey, you are talking about a couple of years ago."

DR. S: Well, what we need to work on is to bring back the sense of youthful middle age.

MRS. A: I don't think that will ever come back. I always felt inside that I was about 19 or 20 and now I feel 60 years old. I said we could talk to you and tell you anything. You have taught us a great deal, and not to worry about recriminations.

MR. A: There were times when I felt that you were trying to make her mad at you.

DR. S: I never did that. I have always liked you.

MRS. A: I always felt that you liked me. It was that feeling. I remember the look on your face when I showed you her picture. I will never forget it.

DR. S: I can't describe what went through me.

MRS. A: You showed it. It was like hitting you, and you absolutely recoiled as though I had hit you. I miss you when I don't see you.

DR. S: How often do you think we ought to meet now? Should we make the next meeting in a month?

MR. A: They've been almost about a month apart.

MRS. A: I would hate to think about our meetings finishing, ending.

Principles of Postvention

What can be noted in this exchange are some general principles of postventive work:

1. In working with survivor victims of abrasive death, it is best to begin as soon as possible after the tragedy, within the first 72 hours if that can be managed.
2. Remarkably little resistance is met from the survivors; most are either willing or eager to have the opportunity to talk to a professionally oriented person.
3. Negative emotions about the decedent or about the death itself—irritation, anger, envy, shame, guilt, and so on—need to be explored, but not at the very beginning.
4. The postvener should play the important role of reality tester. He is not so much the echo of conscience as the quiet voice of reason.
5. Medical evaluation of the survivors is crucial. One should be constantly alert for possible decline in physical health and in overall mental well-being.
6. Needless to say, pollyannish optimism or banal platitudes should be avoided—this statement being a good example.
7. Grief work takes a while—from several months (about a year) to the end of the life, but certainly more than three months or six sessions.
8. A comprehensive program of health care on the part of a benign and enlightened community (or a first-rate hospital) should include preventive, interventive, and *postventive* elements.

References

Bowlby J: Processes of mourning. Int J Psychoanal, 42:317-340, 1961

Caplan G: Principles of Preventive Psychiatry. New York, Basic Books, 1964

Freud S: Mourning and melancholia, in the Standard Edition of the Complete Psychological Works of Sigmund Freud, vol. 14. London, Hogarth, 1957

Friedman P, Lum L: Some psychiatric notes on the *Andrea Doria* disaster. Am J Psychiatry, 114:426-432, 1957

Kraus A, Lilienfeld A: Some epidemiologic aspects of the high mortality rate in the young widowed group. J Chronic Dis, 10:207-217, 1959

Lifton R: Death in Life: Survivors of Hiroshima. New York, Vintage, 1969
Lindemann E: Symptomatology and management of acute grief. Am J Psychiatry, 101:141-148, 1944
Lindemann E, Greer I: A study of grief: Emotional responses to suicide, in Cain A (ed): Survivors of Suicide. Springfield, Ill., Thomas, 1972
Lindemann E, Vaughn WT, McGinnis M: Preventive intervention in a four-year-old child whose father committed suicide, in Cain A (ed): Survivors of Suicide. Springfield, Ill., Thomas, 1972
Parkes C: Bereavement and mental illness. Br J Med Psychology, 38:1-26, 1964
Parkes C: The first year of bereavement. Psychiatry, 33:442-467, 1970
Parkes C: Psychosocial transitions: A field for study. Social Sci Med, 5:101-115, 1971
Parkes C: Bereavement. New York, International Universities Press, 1972
Parkes C, Fitzgerald R: Broken heart: A statistical study of increased mortality among widowers. Br Med J, 1:740-743, 1969
Rahe RH: Subjects' recent life changes and their near-future illness reports. Ann Clin Res, 4:250-265, 1972
Rees W, Lutkins S. Mortality of bereavement. Br Med J, 4:13-16, 1967
Shneidman ES: Suicide, sleep and death, J Consult Psychol, 28:95-106, 1964
Shneidman ES: Recent developments in suicide prevention, in Shneidman ES (ed): The Psychology of Suicide. New York, Science House, 1970
Shneidman ES: Death sof Man. New York, Penguin, 1974
Silverman P: Intervention with the widow of a suicide, in Cain A (ed): Survivors of Suicide. Springfield, Ill., Thomas, 1972
Stein Z, Susser M: Widowhood and mental illness. Br J Prev Soc Med, 23:106-110, 1969
Varah C: The Samaritans. New York, Macmillan, 1966
Wallace A: Tornado in Worcester: An Exploratory Study of Individual and Community Behavior in an Extreme Situation. Washington, DC, National Research Council, 1956
Weisman AD: On Dying and Denying. New York, Behavioral Publications, 1972
Wolfenstein M: Disaster: A Psychological Essay. New York, Macmillan, 1957
Young M, Benjamin B, Wallis C: The mortality of widowers, Lancet, 2:454-456, 1963

Acknowledgments

Grateful acknowledgment is made to the following for permission to reprint:

Aldine-Atherton for "Orientations toward Death" in Robert W. White (Ed.), *The Study of Lives* (1963).
Brunner/Mazel, Inc. for "Psychotherapy with Suicidal Patients" in T.B. Karasu and L. Bellak (Eds.), *Specialized Techniques in Individual Psychotherapy* (1980).
California Department of Health for "The Logical Environment of Suicide" in *California's Health*, May 15, 1960, Vol. 17, No. 22, pp. 193-196.
Encyclopaedia Britannica for "Suicide" in *Encyclopaedia Britannica*, 14th edition, (1973).
Grune and Stratton, Inc. for "Postvention: Care of the Bereaved" in R.O. Pasnau (Ed.), *Consultation-Liaison Psychiatry* (1975).
Harper and Row, Inc. for "Self-Destruction: Suicide Notes and Tragic Lives" in E.S. Shneidman, *Voices of Death* (1980).
Human Sciences Press for "Perturbation and Lethality as Precursors of Suicide in a Gifted Group" (retitled "Suicide among the Gifted") in *Life-Threatening Behavior* (1971, Vol. 1, pp. 23-45).
Insight Publishing Company for "A Psychological Theory of Suicide" in *Psychiatric Annals* (1977, Vol. 7, pp. 25-40).
U.S. Department of Health, Education and Welfare for "The Psychological Autopsy" in L.I. Gottschalk *et al* (Eds.), *Guide to the Investigation and Reporting of Drug Abuse Deaths* (1977).
John Wiley and Sons, Inc. for "Logical Content Analysis" in G. Gerbner *et al* (Eds.), *The Analysis of Communication Content* (1969).

Name Index

The page numbers in this index refer to the numbers set in
brackets on each page.

Subject Index

Aggression, in suicide 12
Alcoholism, and suicide 72, 83, 84
Altruistic suicide 11
Ambivalence, in suicide 12, 14, 29, 34, 35, 39, 43, 106, 155
Anomic suicide 11
Appropriate death 61
Artists and authors, suicide of 22-23
Aspects of reasoning, in suicide 110-114
Attempted suicide, characteristics of 16-17

Befriending 158
Bereavement 157
"Burning out" 74, 75, 81

"Catalogical suicides" 91-92
Cemeteries 106
Cessation, idea of, in suicide 29, 33, 38, 41, 152
Christian attitudes toward suicide 10
Clues to suicide 62, 69-71
Cognitive maneuvers, in suicide 108, 110, 115
Community resources, use of, for suicidal person 155
Confidentiality, in suicide work 156
Constriction, in suicide 29, 32-33, 35, 38, 39, 98, 99, 152
Consultation, use of 155
Contra-logic 122-124
Continuation 43-44
Contraintention 52-54
Conversation, rules of 151, 160-162
Crisis intervention, and suicide prevention 26, 27, 156

Death, and suicide 15-16
Death certificate, suggestions for improvement of 143-148
Death Investigation Team 137
Death phenomena, classification of 47-53
Depression 60, 72, 104-105
"Dialectical suicidology" 96
Dichotomous thinking, in suicide notes 32, 38, 92-93, 96

Disaster, and death 159
Drug-related deaths 134, 139-140
Dyadic nature of suicide 14, 155
The Dwarf 100-103

Egoistic suicide 11
Emotions,
  in grief 158, 159, 160, 162, 163-166
  in suicide 12, 13, 96, 97, 149
Enlightenment position on suicide 10
Equivocal death 26, 133, 134

Fallacies, logical, in suicide 90-93, 109
Father, role of in suicide 12, 69, 81, 84

Grief 158

Hara-kiri 11, 21
Homosexuality, in suicide 72
Hopelessness, in suicide 11, 13, 44, 81, 97
Hospitalization, in suicide 155
Hostility (see Aggression)

Idio-logic 110-112
Idiosyncrasies of thinking 110-114
Indirect suicide 54-61
Inimicality, in suicide 29, 30-31, 37, 152
Instability, and suicide 81, 83
Intention, in suicide and death 134
Intentioned death 8, 45-47
International Classification of Diseases and Causes of Death 133
Interruption states 43
Isolation, in suicide 36

Law, and suicide 19-20
Lethality, in suicide 13, 27, 34, 62, 149, 150, 153
  on death certificate 141, 145
Lethality scale 145
Life chart 68-72
Locus of blame in suicide 10-11
Logic of suicide 90-93, 108-132
"Logical suicides" 90